RETIREMENT
THE FINAL FRONTIER

KELLY SHAW

This document discusses general concepts for retirement planning, and is not intended to provide tax or legal advice. Individuals are urged to consult with their tax and legal professionals regarding these issues. This handbook should ensure that clients understand a) that annuities and some of their features have costs associated with them; b) that income received from annuities is taxable; and c) that annuities used to fund IRAs do not afford any additional measure of tax deferral for the IRA owner.

Printed in the United States of America

First Printing, 2015

Gradient Positioning Systems, LLC
4105 Lexington Avenue North, Suite 110
Arden Hills, MN 55126 (877) 901-0894

Contributors: Nick Stovall, Nate Lucius, Mike Binger and Gradient Positioning Systems, LLC

TABLE OF CONTENTS

INTRODUCTION

"Space… The final frontier…
These are the voyages of the Starship Enterprise.
Its continuing mission: to explore strange new worlds;
to seek out new life; new civilizations…
To boldly go where no one has gone before!"
*   – Captain James T. Kirk, Star Trek: The Original Series*

The opening words to the science fiction Star Trek series and later films in many ways represent what retirement means for the Boomer generation today: a journey into the great unknown.

Retirement is a wholly different time in your life, and Boomers are a different kind of retiree. Our generation has provided for our kids, bought them cars, sent them to college, and in some cases even brought them back into our homes when they couldn't find jobs. As you retire, you are said to be entering the golden sunset years. But what if you want to go beyond the day-to-day rigors to discover new frontiers? What if you want to shoot for the stars?

My own mother was 26 years old when we came to America, and I remember how her parents—my grandparents—had white hair and easy chairs, with plastic coverings on the formal living room couch. Today's retirees aren't sitting around in chairs. We are all about an active retirement. At 60, we feel and look and act like we are in our 20s and 30s, and after a lifetime of taking care of business, we're ready for an adventure. Whether it's golfing, doing volunteer work or spending time with the grandkids, a Boomer retirement is about doing what you love, and as a fellow Boomer myself, I want to help you fund the lifestyle you've earned and the adventures you crave.

You may have heard a lot of negative things about the state of the world today: the low interest rates on bank CDs, the volatility of the market and the likelihood of a tax increase. All things considered, if you have spent your lifetime working a lot and saving a little, there's no reason you can't embark on the retirement of your designing. If you think of retirement as a journey into the unknown, then you'll understand the need for a good vehicle—like a starship—that can safely transport you through the years. In the case of retirement planning, the Starship Enterprise is your solid and well-constructed PLAN.

WELCOME TO THE RETIREMENT ENTERPRISE

Retirement is a journey into the future. For some of us, it might be a short journey; for others, it could be as long as 35 or 40 years. The fuel of your retirement enterprise is the money that you have been working so hard to save and invest, and your goal as you launch into this new phase of life is to be able to do all the things you have been waiting and wanting to do. For most retirees, the biggest fear is running out of money. This fear can be compared to a ship in deep space with no gas stations in sight. How long will you be able to keep going?

Once you stop working and are no longer drawing a paycheck, refueling your bank accounts also becomes a lot more difficult. That variable of an unknown distance—the vastness of space which represents an unknown number of years ahead of you—is what puts a real test on the endurance of your money and its ability to provide for you.

Worrying about your money is a reality for many, but it doesn't have to be. *The question isn't CAN you or SHOULD you put your money to work for you and your family. It's HOW.*

Money represents more than the paper it's printed on. It is the embodiment of your time, your talents, and your commitments. It buys the food you eat, the house you sleep in, the car you drive, and the clothes you wear. It also helps provide you with the lifestyle you want to live once you retire.

The truth is that it takes more than just money to fulfill your retirement needs and desires. Your income, your plans for retirement, your future healthcare expenses, and the continued accumulation of your assets after you stop working and drawing a paycheck all rely on one thing: *You.* How you approach your finances today determines whether or not those assets you have accumulated can support you for the duration of tomorrows that make up your retirement journey.

Most retirees and aspiring retirees think of their retirement savings in terms of an investment whose purpose is to generate high returns. While this way of thinking was appropriate during your working and accumulation years, it no longer applies once you enter into the deep space of your retirement years. Why? *Because the purpose of your savings during retirement changes.* The purpose of your savings during retirement is to support you. It is the fuel that funds your journey and provides for your daily needs. As such your focus now should switch away from growth and onto safety. You want to preserve what you have, because once you launch into retirement, you no longer have the time or opportunity to make up for deep losses.

Enter the retirement plan. A comprehensive plan takes into consideration all the assets you have currently accumulated and strategizes for efficient distribution. Your distribution years are the opposite of your accumulation years. Instead of putting money into your accounts, you are taking money out. Instead of earning, you are spending. What needs to happen before you launch into retirement space is a preservation and maximization of all your assets, including Social Security and tax strategies, which is why a retirement portfolio looks different than an investment portfolio geared for the accumulation years. While growth is a component of retirement planning, it is the safety of your nest egg that determines whether or not it can support you for the long journey ahead. Looking at your investments in terms of their ability to safely and consistently generate income means taking advantage of new products and investment tools you may not have considered before. It also means taking advantage of the programs and solutions offered to today's retirees.

One such solution often overlooked by Boomers, myself included, is Social Security. If done right, your Social Security benefit can provide a much larger portion of your income than you might think. Not only does it provide you with a guaranteed paycheck, but these payments are regularly increased to counter inflation, which means you get regular infusions of fuel into your enterprise tank. I've found in my practice that if you factor in this cost of living adjustment at a 2.8 percent average rate and capitalize on filing options, the average Boomer couple can generate about the same amount of income from their Social Security benefit as they might from a million dollar investment portfolio. This is a benefit that you've already paid into your entire working life, which is why we have dedicated an entire chapter of this book to this one subject alone. Don't make the mistake of claiming too early just because it's easy.

Claiming your Social Security benefit at the wrong time is one of the most common mistakes retirees make, but it's certainly not the only one. Your retirement enterprise has many working parts, and as such, there is more than one thing that can go wrong.

AVOIDING THE BLACK HOLES

My father retired as a 30-year veteran of the United States Air Force, and in 1982 he was one of the healthiest, most athletic men I have ever known. It was a shock to us all when at the age of 62, he had a stroke followed by a heart attack that left him in a semi-comatose condition.

For the first six months, the Veteran's Administration took care of my dad, but after that, we were on our own. My father's strong heart continued to function even after he was taken off life support. The nursing staff continued to hydrate and feed him, and he stayed alive in this semi-comatose condition for another seven years. During that time he endured nine bouts of pneumonia and went from 210 pounds of lean muscle to 89 pounds of withering flesh. The information we got as far as planning for the expense and getting our affairs in order was about 95 percent correct. The 5 percent that we got wrong was what cost my parents everything they owned. My mom used all her resources to cover the cost of my dad's long term care, and eventually, she lost everything.

I got into the business of asset protection and retirement planning to help make sure that what happened to my family doesn't happen to you. In the 24 years I've been in the business, one thing has become remarkably clear: **Doing the right things *before* retirement can become completely obliterated if you don't take the steps to *preserve what you have* prior to or during retirement.**

Working with a financial professional trained in this area can help you avoid the most damaging mistakes made by retirees today. These mistakes are like black holes that can swallow up everything you own, leaving both yourself and the people you love with nothing but empty spaces.

Mistake #1: Not having a clear picture of what you want your retirement to look like. What do you want to be doing during your retirement years? What are your Big Audacious Goals? Not understanding what your money is there for often leads to its mismanagement. If you do with your money what you have always done (investing it for growth in the stock market) or follow outdated advice (such as taking out at a five percent distribution rate), you increase the chances that you *will* run out of that money. Those chances increase significantly if a stock market loss occurs during the early years of your retirement, while you are making withdrawals on those funds.

Mistake #2: Not having an income plan in place to fund that retirement dream. The Color of Money outlined in Chapter Two gives you a visual schematic so you can *see* if your current investments are in alignment with your big audacious goals. Organizing your nest egg this way gives you the opportunity to preserve your lifestyle first so that when a market correction comes along, your income stays intact.

Market loss isn't the only risk out there, however, which is why a comprehensive income plan also considers taxes, inflation risk and longevity.

Mistake #3: Not addressing longevity issues. The medical community, doctors and scientists have put us in a position now where our life expectancy is getting further and further out. Obviously this is a good thing for Boomers with a robust determination to do it all during retirement, but we have to remember that the longer we live, the more it will cost us. According to the Social Security administration, the average man in 1950 lived to be 65 years old, and the average woman lived to be 71. Today, men are living an average of 19 years longer and women an average of 15 years longer, which means if you retire at age 65 today, you need to plan for at least 20 more years of income.*

A good income plan factors in longevity. This includes looking at your family's life expectancy and addressing long term and health care needs.

Today's retirees have more than one choice when it comes to paying for the cost of long term care, and we will be covering these options in this book, including the little-known benefit funded by Congress called Aid and Attendance. As the spouse of a wartime veteran, had my mom been able to access this benefit, her lifestyle during retirement would have been vastly improved.

The financial professional who helped you during your earning years may have done a good job with your growth portfolio, but during your distribution years, you want to find someone in the business of income planning. Anybody can learn how to drive a car. During retirement, you want a professional who can captain a starship.

THIS IS YOUR CAPTAIN SPEAKING

It is our mission at SAVE Inc. Financial to help you achieve a comfortable, safe and worry-free retirement even as you journey into the great unknown. Our core specialties are helping Boomers to generate income and maximize their Social Security. When your investments are structured in vehicles designed to provide you with returns that combat inflation and market volatility, and when your plan has contingencies that provide for longevity risks, then your enterprise is shielded. We'll take care of handling all the details so you can embark on the adventures important to you without having to worry about the safety of your money.

---

* *http://www.ncbi.nlm.nih.gov/books/NBK62373/*

Having a retirement plan is about more than just organizing your assets. To quote Captain Kirk from the original Star Trek series, having a plan can help your dream become *a reality that spreads throughout the stars.*

– Kelly Shaw, President and Owner of Save Inc. Financial

1
FIRST CONTACT

"Seize the time. Live now. Make now always the most precious time. Now will never come again."
— *Captain Jean-Luc Picard, Star Trek: The Next Generation*

Will your Social Security benefit, savings and other retirement assets be enough? If you're like Scott and Janice, you hope so. When the couple turned 60 years old, they started thinking about what their lives would be like in the next 10 years. When would they retire? What would their retirement look like? How much money did they have?

They could both count on Social Security benefits, but neither one really knew how much their monthly checks would be, or when to file for them. Scott had a modest pension that he could begin collecting at age 67. He had always hoped to retire before that age. Janice had a 401(k), but she honestly wasn't exactly sure how it worked, how she could draw money from it and how much income it would provide once she retired.

While Scott and Janice may sound like they're totally in the dark about their retirement, the truth is there are a lot of people just like them. They know retirement is coming and know they have some assets to rely on, but they aren't sure how it will all come together to provide them with a retirement income.

You spend your entire working life hoping what you put into your retirement accounts will help you live comfortably once you clock out of the workforce for good. The key word in that sentiment and the word that can make retirement feel like a looming problem instead of a rewarding life stage, is **hope**. You hope you'll have enough money.

The question on most retirees' minds isn't can I retire, but can I retire and do what I want to do, when I want to do it? Leaving your retirement up to chance is unadvisable by nearly any standard, yet millions of people find themselves *hoping* instead of planning for a happy ending. Retirement is a precious time, an opportunity for you to do all the things you couldn't do when work and family life consumed the bulk of your time. An income plan designed for you should support your likes, dislikes and your hopes for the future years. Your personal goals come *before* the assets because until we know what you want your retirement to look like, we can't make recommendations for you.

EMBARKING ON YOUR JOURNEY

Today's retirees have redefined what it means to be retired. Answers to the question, 'what does retirement mean to you?' are as varied as the individual, spanning the gambit from starting a business to spending time with the grandkids. Imagine that you own a pair of ruby slippers like ones Dorothy wore in The Wizard of Oz. If you could click your heels together and go anywhere in the world (or out of this world,) where would you want to go? What does home mean to you? Who are the people you'd like to be with? And how will you be spending your time?

While it seems logical that a retirement plan should begin with questions about money, we like to start by asking questions about you and your life. What are your likes and dislikes, your hopes and your dreams? What do you want to do with your time during retirement? A good financial planner will look at all the things important to you and ask the question, 'what are we trying to accomplish with your money?' What are your goals? And what are the pros and cons associated with the financial side of those goals? Then taking this even further, they will help you to discover ways to alleviate the negative consequences that might occur as a result of these goals.

> *James met with his financial professional and told him, "I want to take $20,000 out of my IRA."*

The financial professional knew that James had an IRA that was earning an 8 percent return, and he knew that taking out $20,000 would cause a tax event for James, increasing his tax bracket. In order for James to net $20,000 from his IRA after taxes, he would have to pull out closer to $30,000. So the financial professional asked him, "Why? Why do you want to take $20,000 out of your IRA?"

"Because I want to buy a car," James answered.

"Okay," said the professional, "You want to buy a car, but the interest rates on car loans right now range from 0 to 2 percent."

"Oh, I don't want a car loan," James explained, "Not while I'm retired."

"And why is that?"

"Because I don't want to have to worry about making a payment. What if I'm on a cruise in Alaska? Or bicycling across Europe? I don't want the worry."

"Okay, well I can understand that," said the professional. "Let's see if there is a way we can achieve your objective without increasing your taxes."

The financial professional came up with a plan for the long term. He arranged for $5,000 to be transferred out of the IRA for a down payment on the vehicle James wanted, which qualified him for a zero percent interest loan. By only transferring out $5,000, James avoided a tax consequence. The monthly payments for the car amounted to $490. They set up a direct deposit from the IRA to his bank account for the amount of $550 and had the payment deducted automatically so that James never received a bill. By moving out the money in smaller quantities, the tax repercussions were also smaller, and James was able to achieve his objective: a new car without having to worry about car payments!

WHAT DO YOU WANT TO ACCOMPLISH?

When the time comes for retirement, you want your money to provide you with a comfortable lifestyle and stable income after your working days are done. You might also have other desires, such as traveling, purchasing property, or moving to be closer to your family (or farther away.) You may also want your assets to provide for your loved ones after you are gone.

A comprehensive plan looks at the bigger picture of what you want to accomplish and why. We start with questions about who you are, where you are and what you want to do, because all of this directly impacts your income needs, your plans for retirement and your future healthcare expenses. There is nothing wrong with taking out $30,000 from your IRA as long as you understand the repercussions. Most retirees don't want to outlive their retirement savings. Asking, *what is the purpose of this money?* will help you make the most out of your financial decisions, so you can accomplish your goals while maintaining your lifestyle.

From a purely financial perspective, the primary challenge of planning for a long, secure retirement is preparing for the day your paycheck stops and you need to turn a lifetime of savings into an income you cannot outlive. It is something quite unlike any financial challenge you have faced before.

Think of it like this: You took time to choose your career, your educational path, your employment experience, and the time and talent required to develop your professional skill-set. You chose a profession or a line of work that matched your skills and talents with your income needs and lifestyle choices. You did this to suit your needs and preferences, to give you the salary you desired, and to do the work you were interested in and good at performing. Creating a retirement plan requires the same crafting and care that you put into your career. Your assets, your income needs, and your lifestyle are different than your neighbor's, and you need a retirement plan that reflects your needs, not theirs or anyone else's.

NEW IDEAS FOR RETIREMENT

Not all investment products are suitable for producing income, especially in today's low-interest, high market volatility climate. A near-zero percent return on a bank CD may be considered safe in that you can't lose principal, but with outside forces such as inflation and taxes, such a low yield won't sustain your income due to the rapid erosion of your purchasing power. Aggressive equity investments in the stock market can also result in catastrophic loss due to volatile market downturns.

The reality is that investment strategies and savings plans that worked in the past have encountered challenging new circumstances that have turned them on their heads. The Great

Recession of the early 2000's highlighted how old investment ideas were not only ineffective but incredibly destructive to the retirement plans of millions of Americans, teaching us that not understanding where your money is invested (and the potential risk of those investments) can work against you. The dawn of an entirely restructured health care system brings with it new options and challenges that will undoubtedly change the way insurance companies provide investment products and services. Saving and investing money isn't enough to truly get the most out of it. You must have a planful approach to managing your assets that refocuses the purpose of your savings away from the return rate and onto what the money was put away for: income.

Identify the purpose of your money. Instead of chasing returns and worrying about how much you can earn, focus on income creation. Think of your 401(k) as your future pension, or the fuel that will power your retirement enterprise. Leaving that tank of money in the market or using it for an emergency fund means you could find yourself in serious trouble if the market takes another hit like it did in 2008. What worked for your parents or even your parents' parents was probably good advice back then when it came to equity investments. It used to be that a 6 percent was considered a safe withdrawal rate. Today's safe withdrawal rates are closer to 2 or 3 percent, and even when following that rule, a bad market combined with those distributions can put you in peril of outliving your money. People in retirement or approaching retirement today need new ideas and professional guidance. The first step to refocusing your investments begins with identifying how much risk your current investments are exposed to.

HOPE SO VS. KNOW SO MONEY

Let's take a look at some of the basic truths about money as it relates to saving for retirement. There are essentially two kinds of money: *Hope So* and *Know So*. Everyone can divide their money into these two categories. Some have more of one kind than the other. The goal is to ensure that the funds you are relying on for income are safe and balanced according to your individual needs. Hope So Money is money that is at risk. It fluctuates with the market. It has no minimum guarantee. It is subject to investor activity, stock prices, market trends, buying trends, etc. You get the picture. This money is exposed to more risk but also has the potential for more reward. Because the market is subject to change, you can't really be sure what the value of your investments will be worth in the future. You can't really *rely* on it at all. For this reason, we refer to it as Hope So Money. This doesn't mean you shouldn't have some money invested in the market, but it would

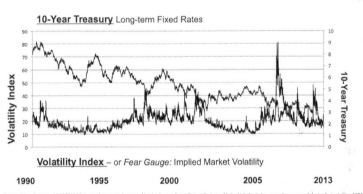

10-Year Treasury Long-term Fixed Rates

Volatility Index – or *Fear Gauge:* Implied Market Volatility

Source: Yahoo Finance – 12-31-2013. VIX is a trademarked ticker symbol for the Chicago Board Options Exchange Market Volatility Index, a popular measure of the implied volatility of S&P 500 index options. Often referred to as the fear index or the fear gauge, it represents one measure of the market's expectation of stock market volatility over the next 30 day period. (wikipedia.com) The CBOE 10-year Treasury Note (TNX) is based on 10 times the yield-to-maturity on the most recently auctioned 10-year Treasury note. Past performance does not guarantee future results. Some illustrations may show how a market index has performed. An investor cannot invest in an index, although there are some investments designed to mirror index performance. Past performance is not a guarantee of future results.

The VIX, or volatility index, of the market represents expected market volatility. When the VIX drops, economic experts expect less volatility. When the VIX rises, more volatility is expected.

1. *VIX is a trademarked ticker symbol for the Chicago Board Options Exchange (CBOE) Market Volatility Index, a popular measure of the implied volatility of S&P 500 index options. Often referred to as the fear index or the fear gauge, it represents one measure of the market's expectation of stock market volatility over the next 30 day period. (wikipedia.com)*

2. *The CBOE 10-Year Treasury Note (TNX) is based on 10 times the yield-to-maturity on the most recently auctioned 10-year Treasury note.*

be dangerous to assume you can know what it will be worth in the future.

Hope So Money is an important element of a retirement plan, especially in the early stages of planning when you can trade volatility for potential returns, and when a longer investment timeframe is available to you. In the long run, time can smooth out the ups and downs of money exposed to the market. Working with a professional and leveraging a long-term investment strategy has the potential to create rewarding returns from Hope So Money.

Know So Money, on the other hand, is safer when compared to Hope So Money. Know So Money is made up of dependable, low-risk or no-risk money, and investments that you can count on. Social Security is one of the most common forms of Know So Money. Income you draw or will draw from Social Security is guaranteed. You have paid into Social Security your entire career, and you can rely on that money during your retirement. Unlike the market, rates of growth for Know So Money are dependent on 10-year treasury rates. The 10-year treasury, or TNX, is commonly considered to represent a very secure and safe place for your money, hence Know So Money. The 10-year treasury drives key rates for things such as mortgage rates or CD rates. Know So Money may not be as exciting as Hope So Money, but it is safer. You can be fairly sure you will have it in the future.

Knowing the difference between Hope So and Know So Money is an important step towards a successful retirement plan. People who are 55 or older and who are looking ahead to retirement should be relying on more Know So Money than Hope So Money.

Ideally, the rates of return on Hope So and Know So Money would have an overlapping area that provided an acceptable rate of risk for both types of money. In the early 1990s, interest rates were high and market volatility was low. At that time, you could invest in either Hope So or Know So Money options because the rates of return were similar from both Know So and Hope So investments, and you were likely to be fairly successful with a wide range of investment options. At that time, you could expose yourself to an acceptable amount of risk or an acceptable fixed rate. Basically, it was difficult to make a mistake during that time period. Today, you don't have those options. Market volatility is at all-time highs while interest rates are at all-time lows. They are so far apart from each other that it is hard to know what to do with your money.

Yesterday's investment rules may not work today. Not only could they hamper achieving your goals, they may actually harm your financial situation. We are currently in a period when the rates for Know So Money options are at historic lows, and the volatility of Hope So Money is higher than ever. There is no overlapping acceptable rate, making both options less than ideal. *Because of this uncertain financial landscape, wise investment strategies are more important now than ever.*

This unique situation requires fresh ideas and investment tools that haven't been relied on in the past. Investing the way your parents did will not pay off. The majority of investment ideas used by financial professionals in the 1990s aren't applicable to today's markets. That kind of investing will likely get you in trouble and compromise your retirement. Today, you need a better PLAN.

HOW MUCH RISK ARE YOU EXPOSED TO?

Many investors don't know how much risk they are exposed to. It is helpful to organize your assets so you can have a clear under-standing of how much of your money is at risk and how much is in safer holdings. This process starts with listing all your assets. Let's take a look at the two kinds of money:

Hope So Money is, as the name indicates, money that you *hope* will be there when you need it. Hope So Money represents what you would like to get out of your investments. Examples of Hope So Money include:

- Stock market funds, including index funds
- Mutual funds
- Variable annuities
- REITS

Know So Money is money that you know you can count on. It is safer money that isn't exposed to the level of volatility as the asset types noted above. You can more confidently count on having this money when you need it. Examples of Know So Money are:

- Government backed bonds
- Savings and checking accounts
- Fixed income annuities
- CDs
- Treasuries
- Money market accounts

> » *Saavik had a modest brokerage account that he added to when he could. When he changed jobs a couple years ago, at age 58, Saavik transferred his 401(k) assets into an IRA. Just a few years from retirement, he is now beginning to realize that nearly every dollar he has saved for retirement is subject to market risk.*
>
> *Intuitively, he knows that the time has come to shift some assets to an alternative that is safer, but how much is the right amount?*

How do you determine how much risk your assets should be exposed to? Where do you begin? Luckily, there's a simple guideline or starting point you can use to start making decisions about risk management. It's called the Rule of 100.

THE RULE OF 100

While there is no single approach to investment risk determination advice that is universally applicable to everyone, there are some helpful guidelines. One of the most useful is called *The Rule of 100*. The Rule of 100 is a general rule that helps shape asset diversification* for the average investor. The rule states that the number 100 minus an investor's age equals the amount of assets they should have exposed to risk.

The Rule of 100: 100 - (your age) = the percentage of your assets that should be exposed to risk (Hope So Money).

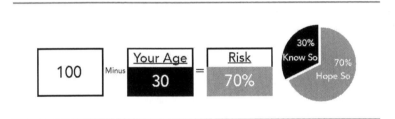

For example, if you are a 30-year-old investor, the Rule of 100 would indicate that you should be focusing on investing primarily in the market and taking on a substantial amount of risk in your portfolio. The Rule of 100 suggests that 70 percent of your investments should be exposed to risk.

100 - (30 years of age) = 70 percent

Asset Diversification disclosure – Diversification and asset allocation does not assure or guarantee better performance and cannot eliminate the risk of investment loss. Before investing, you should carefully read the applicable volatility disclosure for each of the underlying funds, which can be found in the current prospectus.

Now, not every 30-year-old should have exactly 70 percent of their assets in mutual funds and stocks. The Rule of 100 is based on your chronological age, not your "financial age," which could vary based on your investment experience, your aversion or acceptance of risk and other factors. While this rule isn't an ironclad solution to anyone's finances, it's a pretty good place to start.

Once you've taken the time to look at your assets with a professional to determine your risk exposure, you can use the Rule of 100 to make changes that put you in a more stable investment position—one that reflects your comfort level.

Much of the flexibility that comes with investing earlier in life is related to *compounding*. Compounded earnings can be incredibly powerful over time. The longer your money has time to compound, the greater your wealth will be. This is what most people talk about when they refer to putting their money to work. This is also why the Rule of 100 favors risk for the young. If you start investing when you are young, you can invest smaller amounts of money in a more aggressive fashion because you have the potential to make a profit in a rising market and you can harness the power of compounding earnings. When you are 40, 50 or 60 years old, that potential becomes less and less and you are forced to have more money at lower amounts of risk to realize the same returns. **It basically becomes more expensive to prudently invest the older you get.**

Risk tolerance generally reduces as you get older. If you are 40 years old and lose 30 percent of your portfolio in a market downturn this year, you have 20 or 30 years to recover it. If you are 68 years old, you have five to 10 years (or less) to make the same recovery. That new circumstance changes your whole retirement perspective. At age 68, it's likely that you simply aren't as interested in suffering through a tough stock market. There is less time to recover from downturns, and the stakes are higher. The money you have saved is money you will soon need to provide you with income, or is money that you already need to meet your income demands.

The Rule of 100 can apply to overarching financial management and to specific investment products that you own as well. Take the 401(k) for example. Many people have them, but not many people understand how their money is allocated within their 401(k). An employer may have someone who comes in once a year and explains the models and options that employees can choose from, but that's as much guidance as most 401(k) holders get. Many 401(k) options include target date funds that change their risk exposure over time, essentially following a form of the Rule of 100. Selecting one of these options can often be a good move for employees because they shift your risk as you age, securing more Know So Money when you need it.

Ultimately, you are the only person who can answer the question, *what is your risk tolerance.* Everyone has their own level of comfort. Your risk tolerance will be based on your values and attitudes, what you had to sacrifice to get to where you are today, and your income goals during retirement. A financial professional can look at your assets with you and discuss alternatives to optimize your balance between Know So and Hope So Money.

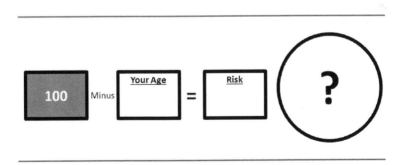

CHAPTER 1 RECAP //

- Having a planful approach to retirement begins with the retirement goals of you, the investor. What do you want to be doing during your retirement? What is the purpose of your money? Most retirees find they are stuck thinking of their investments in terms of the returns they produce rather than in terms of the income they can produce. The purpose of your savings during retirement is to generate income for you.

- The rules for retirement planning have changed. Investing the way your parents did will not pay off and the majority of investment ideas used by financial professionals in the 1990s aren't applicable to today's markets.

- Understanding where and how your assets are invested is key to understanding and securing the safety of your principal. There is money you hope you'll have in the future, and there's money you know you'll have in the future. With the help of a financial professional, it's easy to see what percentages of your assets are invested in risk, Hope So Money, and safe, Know So Money.

- Use the Rule of 100 as a general guiding principle when determining how much risk your retirement investments should be exposed to (100 - [your age] = [percentage of your investments that can comfortably exposed to risk]).

- Your retirement timeline, income goals and savings will help you determine the amount of risk that is appropriate for you.

FACING THE BORG:
ENCOUNTERS WITH
RETIREMENT RISK

"Resistance is futile."

— *The Borg, Star Trek: Deep Space Nine*

The main threat in the Star Trek series was a fictional alien race known as The Borg. The risks of a Borg encounter included abduction, injections and mind control. Ironically, the ultimate goal of the Borg was to achieve perfection. This can be compared to the habit of investors looking to achieve the perfect rate of return. During your retirement, chasing such perfect returns exposes your money to a threat on par with a Borg encounter: the risk of outliving your money.

» *Lieutenant Uhura had $300,000 invested in her 401(k) plan and another $300,000 in a non-qualified account from telephone stock that she had gotten over the years through her employer. In 1998, she went to talk to a financial professional who specialized in retirement income planning because she wanted to retire early. He proposed she move $300,000 into an investment that would guarantee her principal, giving her safety with an upside, so she could preserve a portion of the money she would soon be relying on for income. Her argument against this was that telephone stock had always done well, and she wanted to leave her money there.*

"I've got almost half a million dollars here," she surmised, "I'm 67 years old. I should be fine!" Lieutenant Uhura went back to her stock broker who kept her heavily invested in things that are good during the accumulations years, but not so good during retirement.

Uhura retired early without maximizing her Social Security. At the age of 62, she started taking out an income distribution of $30,000 a year. Along came the market downturn of 2000 and her telephone stocks took a dive. But Uhura still had bills to pay. She continued to take out the $30,000 annually that she needed for her income. In 2002, her $300,000 401(k) account was down to $120,000, and her other account was down to $140,000. Under the advice of her stock broker, she stayed in her stock market investments, hoping to make back her loses.

At the end of 2008, Lieutenant Uhura called the office of the first financial professional in a panic. What had once been over half a million dollars in retirement money had dwindled down to just under $160,000. She had to sell her house, get rid of her furniture and rent out a small, single bedroom unit because she could no longer afford her lifestyle.

While the above story uses a fictional name, it represents the truth of what happened to many retirees who failed to preserve and properly diversify their assets. Had Lieutenant Uhura preserved what she had from the beginning, she would have enjoyed a very comfortable retirement. Instead, the Borg got her, and she is now part of the unhappy collective.

HOW MARKET TIMING IMPACTS YOUR RETIREMENT

There are two main factors which contributed to Uhura's downfall: poor market timing combined with her withdrawal rate. As a retiree, you have some say about your retirement timeline—when you stop working and when you start withdrawing on your savings—but market performance is at the whims of a global economy.

The years just before and just after retirement are when your savings are at their most vulnerable. The chart below shows us how taking a loss due to stock market fluctuations during the early years can significantly damage your portfolio's ability to sustain you for the long journey ahead. This is what's known in the investment world as *the sequence of returns*, and it is completely out of your control. We will talk in more depth about how this can negatively impact your income, but for now, ask yourself, how safe do you want your retirement income to be? For the last 20 years, an annual withdrawal rate of 4 percent has been considered safe and proven to work about 85 percent of the time. To continue our metaphor of comparing retirement to a journey, if you were told that the aircraft you were boarding had an 85 percent chance of landing safely, would you get on the plane? Would you want your spouse to get on that plane? You don't have to leave the security of your retirement up to chance. There is a better way.

Can Market Volatility Impact My Retirement?

Customer Name:	Capt. Kirk	
Investment Amount:	$300,000	
Index to Illustrate:	S&P 500	
Beginning Month/Year:	January - 2000	
Ending Month/Year:	January - 2014	
Annual Income Withdrawal:	5.00%	
Annual Income Withdrawal COLA:	0.00%	

Month	Year	Beginning Value	One-Year Index Return	Change in Value	Annual Withdrawal	Year End Value
January	2000	$300,000	-2.01%	($6,030)	$15,000	$278,970
January	2001	$278,970	-17.28%	($48,206)	$15,000	$215,764
January	2002	$215,764	-24.25%	($52,323)	$15,000	$148,441
January	2003	$148,441	32.13%	$47,694	$15,000	$181,135
January	2004	$181,135	4.42%	$8,006	$15,000	$174,141
January	2005	$174,141	8.38%	$14,593	$15,000	$173,734
January	2006	$173,734	12.34%	$21,439	$15,000	$180,173
January	2007	$180,173	-4.10%	($7,387)	$15,000	$157,786
January	2008	$157,786	-40.10%	($63,272)	$15,000	$79,514
January	2009	$79,514	30.02%	$23,870	$15,000	$88,384
January	2010	$88,384	19.74%	$17,447	$15,000	$90,831
January	2011	$90,831	0.47%	$427	$15,000	$76,258
January	2012	$76,258	15.94%	$12,156	$15,000	$73,414
January	2013	$73,414	18.96%	$13,919	$15,000	$72,333

Total Change in Account Value: -75.89%

Prepared By: Kelvin Shaw On: 10/31/2014

Save, Inc.

The purpose of this illustration is to demonstrate the potential risks of depleting an account when annual withdrawals are combined with market volatility. To demonstrate this potential risk, the illustration shows hypothetical historical results of an account invested in a broad stock market index. The index values used for the calculations are month-end closing values that are adjusted for dividends and splits. Calculations assume deferral of taxes. The Standard & Poors 500 (S&P 500) is an unmanaged group of securities considered to be representative of the stock market in general. The Dow Jones Industrial Average (DJIA) is a price-weighted average of 30 significant stocks traded on the New York Stock Exchange.

THE COLOR OF MONEY

Throughout our working years, we attempt to accumulate as many eggs as possible into our retirement nest. **Unfortunately, many people focus on *how* to accumulate money without giving any thought to *where* their retirement assets should be invested.** While accumulating your desired amount is important, it is just as important to have your money invested in assets that represent the level of risk or safety that you want. One of the easiest ways to determine where your assets should be allocated is to use a color system for your money.

Each color has unique benefits and features. A properly colored asset allocation can help provide you with the retirement you want, ensuring the fuel in your tank lasts for the duration of your particular journey.

Red Money is risky. There is good growth opportunity with Red Money, but we need to make sure you are prepared for the realities of market volatility. Red doesn't mean that assets are bad, it just means that you should stop, look both directions, and proceed cautiously. Yellow is similar to Red Money and may consider the same types of investments, but benefits from professional management and that can make a significant difference. Professional money management helps ensure that the investment strategy you intend is actually used to make investment decisions. Yellow Money could include portfolios designed to create income, help control volatility, focus on long term growth, or anything in between.

Green Money provides more safety and guarantees. The growth potential is less than Red and Yellow Money, but you are afforded the ability to move comfortably through retirement knowing your assets are safe. This safety means the funds will be available to provide you with the income stream you need.

Over the course of your lifetime, it is likely that you have acquired a variety of assets. Assets can range from money that

Green Money	Red Money
"Green Money" is safer.	"Red Money" is at risk.
This is money that offers a minimum guarantee but it may pose risks other than market risk.	This is money that can go up or down in value. It may pose risk if it is not properly managed to serve a specific purpose in a comprehensive plan.

you have in a savings account or a 401(k), to a pension or an IRA. You have earned money and have made financial decisions based on the best information you had at the time. When viewed as a whole, however, you might not have an overall strategy for the management of your assets. As we have seen from our story example with Lieutenant Uhura, it's more important than ever to know which of your assets are at risk. High market volatility and low treasury rates make for challenging financial topography. Navigating this financial landscape starts with planful asset management that takes into account your specific needs and options.

Even if you feel that you have plenty of money in your 401(k) or IRA, not knowing how much *risk* those investments are exposed to can cause you major financial suffering. This may be the first time you have ever sat down and sorted out all of your assets, allowing you to see how much money you have at risk in the market. Comparing the color of your investments will give you an idea of how near or far you are from adhering to the Rule of 100.

When using the Rule of 100 to calculate your level of risk, your financial age might be different than your chronological age, however. The way you organize your assets depends on your goals and your level of comfort with risk. Whatever you determine the appropriate amount of risk for you to be, you will need to organize your portfolio to reflect your goals. If you have more Red Money than Green Money, in particular, you will need to make decisions about how to move it. You can work with a financial professional to find appropriate Green Money options for your situation.

TYPES OF GREEN MONEY:
LIGHT GREEN AND DARK GREEN

The next step is to know the right amount and ratio of Green and Red Money for you at your stage of retirement planning.

Investing heavily in Red Money and gambling all of your assets on the market is incredibly risky no matter where you fall within the Rule of 100. Money in the market can't be depended on to generate income, and a plan that leans too heavily on Red Money can easily fail, especially when investment decisions are influenced by emotional reactions to market downturns and recoveries. Not only is this an unwise plan, it can be incredibly stressful to an investor who is gambling everything on stocks and mutual funds.

But a plan that uses too much Green Money avoids all volatility and can also fail. Why? Investing all of your money in Certificates of Deposit (CDs), savings accounts, money markets and other low return accounts may provide interest and income, but that likely won't be enough to keep pace with inflation.

Money that you need to depend on for income is Green Money, which is why Green Money becomes much more important as you age. While you want to reduce the amount of Red Money you have and to transition it to Green Money, you don't necessarily need all of it to generate income for you right away. Taking a closer look at Green Money reveals that it comes in two varieties: Dark Green and Light Green Money.

Dark Green Money utilizes investment vehicles that minimize the unknowns. With Dark Green Money, you will always know exactly the minimum and maximum value of your asset on any given day. This gives you the security of knowing how much you will have available for withdrawals, however, as you might imagine, with no unknowns at play your growth potential is limited. This is where Light Green might represent a great alternative.

Light Green Money utilizes investment vehicles that have a growth component. With Light Green Money, you always have a known minimum value, but the maximum potential value may be unknown, and this unknown upside allows for a bit more potential growth. Light Green Money investments can be set for five, ten or even twenty years of growth and may represent income your assets will need to generate for future use. Some investments strategies can also utilize both Light and Dark Green investments.

Whichever variety of Green Money investment you choose, your principal is protected against investment loss.

As you prepare to enter into the distribution phase of your life, organizing your financial nest is important. Do you have your assets allocated properly? When planning for the unknown distance of your retirement journey, it is vital to decide how much of your assets to structure for income now and how much to set for longer term growth with the potential to generate income for future needs.

OPTIMIZING RISK AND FINDING THE RIGHT BALANCE

Determining the amount of risk that is right for you depends on your specific situation. It starts by examining your particular financial position.

The Rule of 100 is a useful way to begin to deliberate the right amount of risk for you, but remember, it's just a baseline. Numbers don't always tell the full story with regards to your risk tolerance. You might be 36 years old and completely risk intolerant. If safe, plodding investments can help you reach your financial goals, then that is what will be best for you. On the other hand, you might be 80 years old with a penchant for playing the market. There are many reasons why someone might be more risk tolerant, not the least of which is feeling young! Experienced investors, people who feel they need to gamble for a higher return, or people who have met their retirement income goals and are looking for additional ways to accumulate wealth are all candidates for investment strategies that incorporate higher levels of risk. In the end, it comes down to your personal tolerance for risk. How much money are you willing to lose?

WHEN NUMBERS LIE

As you prepare your retirement enterprise for its launch off into space, you might look to the numbers to help determine your investment options. Your risk tolerance is an important indicator of what kinds of investments you should consider. Most clients approach retirement with a more conservative investment mindset, yet upon close examination of their assets, they are surprised to learn that they are actually allocated more toward moderately aggressive investments. Why is there such a discrepancy between what they want and what they have?

Aside from the reasons we've already discussed (not having a clear picture of what retirement looks like, what it will cost and how long they will actually live) most investors don't know what type of real return they need or how to set up their portfolios to accomplish that goal. **Looking at the numbers alone doesn't always give you an accurate picture of how much you will earn.** Before embarking on your retirement journey, you want to be clear about these numbers because during retirement, they represent the rocket fuel needed for your tank.

When choosing equity investments, many investors make the mistake of looking at the **average** rate of return rather than the **real** rate of return. The average rate of return can be very misleading to the average investor.

» *Dr. Spock was told about a market investment that would average a 25 percent rate of return. He puts $100,000 of his retirement money into this investment so he can earn an average 25 percent rate of return. During year one, Spock's investment goes up by 100 percent. At the end of the first year, his account value is $200,000.*

During year two things don't go so well, and the account drops by 50 percent. The value of Spock's account after year two is $100,000. During year three, the account grows again *by 100 percent and is back up to $200,000 by the year's end. Come year four, the account loses 50 percent again and Spock's account value drops back down to $100,000.*

*Dr. Spock looks at his investment statement and wonders, what happened to his 25 percent a year? He discovers there is a perfectly logical explanation: according to the numbers, Spock **did** average 25 percent a year. The math of rebounds shows us that it's the real rate of return that matters more to the investor during retirement than the average rate of return.*

Your financial professional may encourage you to be more aggressive with your investment strategy by taking on more risk in order to give you the potential of earning a greater return. Make sure you understand the difference between the average rate of return and the real rate of return before staking the security of your income on an aggressive investment. While the numbers for the rate of return might look good, you will likely be disappointed by the logical outcome of the real rate of return if your income is relying on certain market conditions. As we've stressed earlier, what you want your money to do for you should dictate your choice of investment vehicles.

Proper asset allocation becomes increasingly important as you approach your retirement years. Even if you are unaware of the risk your investments are exposed to, logically speaking, those risks can still drain your assets the way a black hole drains light. These risk factors aren't limited to the sphere of market loss but include other Borgian threats such as rising health care costs and the realities of long term care needs.

THE BLACK HOLES

While no one knows for sure what the future holds, a lot of retirees are finding that their parents are enjoying longer lives than their parents before them. It's not uncommon these days for

Boomers to have parents in their 80s or 90s, which points to the likelihood of their own increased life expectancy. The older you get, the greater the chances that you will keep on living. About one out of every four 65 year-olds can expect to live past the age of 90, and one out of 10 will live past the age of 95.* According to a 2013 article in U.S. Money News, most Americans actually have a pretty good idea of how long they're going to live. They just don't know what to do about it.**

As we live longer and get older, our bodies start to tire and wear out. What happens if you need hip replacement surgery or costly medication? How will you afford the additional expense? The longer we live, the more complicated these health issues become. Sixty-nine percent of people who live to be in their 90s struggle with disability issues that deplete their financial resources.*** These health issues can be like black holes that drain away your funds unless planned for. The trouble is, most people don't want to think about these unpleasant realities, let alone plan for them. As a healthy, optimistic Boomer, you're likely not picturing yourself in a nursing home. Yet according to the U.S. Department of Health and Human Services, **70 percent of people turning age 65 can expect to use some form of long term care during their lives.*****

It might help to understand that long term care extends beyond the scope of nursing home care to include basic custodial services such as cleaning or taking out the garbage, and it can include intrinsic nursing services from the comfort of your own home. The more you plan for the likelihood of this expense, the more options you will have. With a little consideration and the

---

* http://ssa.gov/planners/lifeexpectancy.htm

** http://money.usnews.com/money/blogs/the-best-life/2013/03/13/do-you-recognize-these-lessons-of-longevity

*** http://longtermcare.gov/the-basics/who-needs-care/

guidance of a financial professional, you can find the right tools that fit your income and budget. The following solutions can act like shields to protect your income so when you get bombarded, your retirement lifestyle remains intact.

- **Traditional Long Term Care Insurance**: If you are young enough and you can afford it, long term care insurance allows you to transfer the risk of your long term care expenses onto an insurance company. In exchange for knowing you have contracted protection in place, you pay out an annual premium much like you do with homeowners insurance or car insurance. Long term care insurance becomes more expensive and difficult to qualify for get the older you get; however, the biggest fear most people have regarding this solution is that they will never see the money they paid in. The insurance can only be used to fund long term care costs as set forth by the terms of the contract. While you hope to never need the insurance, if you don't use it, you lose it, as the saying goes. The money might seem to be wasted, but it does buy you peace of mind. Today's retirees have other alternatives.

- **Hybrid Life Insurance Policies with Living Benefits**: More and more people are shying away from the expense of traditional long term care insurance and opting for insurance policies that have benefits in two dimensions built right in. Life insurance companies call long term care benefits Living Benefits because you don't have to die in order to receive the money. The plan provides you with the means to pay for home health care or a nursing home facility *while you are alive*, in addition to the death benefit protection of a life insurance policy. This gives both you and your spouse more options and control of your health care. Most people don't know about this option but Living Benefits have been around for a while and can offer today's Boomers a viable alternative to the problem of funding long term care. The only issue is that your health still has to qualify you for the policy, but since it's a single premium policy the qualifications are relatively simple.

- **Hybrid Indexed Annuities with A Critical Illness Rider:** Many of today's hybrid annuity products have riders that provide an increased income in the event of chronic illness. These riders can also provide income continuation for a surviving spouse in the event of death. This benefit is also known as a home health care doubler, impairment doubler, or an income doubler because the fixed income contracted by the rider will double should you or your spouse require long term care. The inability to perform two out of the six Activities of Daily Living (known as ADLs) triggers the benefit, which can also include funding of basic custodial services such as cleaning and taking out the garbage, or more involved intrinsic nursing services. Qualifying for a critical care rider requires no health exam and no underwriting as long as you can perform all six of the ADLs (which include eating, bathing, dressing, toileting, walking and continence.)

- **Aid and Attendance:** Another way to offset at home health care costs for a large number of veteran Americans is a little known program called Aid and Attendance, which is a supplemental benefit that is paid in addition to a veteran's monthly pension. This solution is available to eligible veterans and to their surviving spouses, provided the spouse remained married to the veteran until death and did not remarry. The program is meant to assist those qualifying individuals who require the regular attendance of another person to assist in bathing, dressing, feeding (not including meal preparation), mobility (assistance with getting in or out of a chair or bed), hygiene (brushing teeth or toileting), and supervision due to cognitive impairment. The veteran or spouse must be paying out of pocket for services which can include care received while residing in an assisted living community or skilled nursing facility and those receiving personal in-home care. In order to qualify for this program the veteran must be eligible to receive a military pension, which means the veteran must meet the following requirements:

- The veteran must have served on active duty for 90 or more consecutive days, with one day occurring during one of the following wartimes:
  - *World War II:* December 7, 1941 through December 31, 1946
  - *Korean War:* June 27, 1950 through January 31, 1955
  - *Vietnam War:* August 5, 1964 (February 28, 1961 for veterans who served in country before August 5, 1964) through May 7, 1975
  - *Gulf War:* August 2, 1990 through a date to be set by law of Presidential Proclamation.*
- The veteran must have received an honorable discharge.
- The veteran must be at least 65 years of age or be totally and permanently disabled.

In addition to the above requirements, the veteran or spouse must also meet certain financial parameters. In general, an applicant must have less than $80,000 in assets, not including the value of their home and/or vehicle(s).**

---

* *http://benefits.va.gov/pension/wartimeperiod.asp*
** *http://www.veteransaidbenefit.org/eligibility_aid_attendance_pension_benefit.htm*

This pension benefit is one of the most misunderstood benefits being administered by the VA today. There are a number of criteria that may affect your eligibility, including your filing time because all benefits are retro-dated back to the date that the VA receives the claim. Talk to your financial professional to find out if you or your family members qualify for this valuable aid.

WORKING WITH A FINANCIAL PROFESSIONAL

Take a moment to think about your income goals:

What is your lifestyle today? Would you like to maintain it into retirement? Are you meeting your needs? Are you happy with your lifestyle? What do you really *need* to live on when you retire?

Some people will have the luxury of maintaining or improving their lifestyle, while others may have to make decisions about what they need versus what they want during their retirement.

Organizing your assets, understanding the color of your money, and creating an income and accumulation plan for retirement can quickly become an overwhelming task. The fact of the matter is that financial professionals build their careers around understanding the different variables affecting retirement financing. Market risk, inflation risk and longevity risks including long term care and medical expenses all seem to be growing at twice the rate of inflation. How do we protect ourselves from all of these risks?

Good planning can put all of these concerns to rest. You might have a million dollar investment portfolio in big company stocks with a proven track record, but your neighbor, who has $300,000 in a diverse investment portfolio that is tailored to their needs may end up enjoying a better retirement lifestyle. Why? They had more than a good work ethic and a penchant for saving. They had a planful approach to retirement asset allocation.

CHAPTER 2 RECAP //

- Assigning colors to money can help you more easily visualize the assets that make up your retirement savings. Green Money is safer and more reliable. Red Money represents assets that are exposed to risk, and Yellow Money is Red Money managed by a professional.
- Outliving your money is what retirees fear the most. Build your retirement income from the sound foundation of Green Money, or Know So Money investments.
- A comprehensive income plan takes into consideration all the risk factors you might encounter during the deep space of your retirement years. Unexpected expenses such as health care can devastate your nest egg if not planned for carefully.
- Statistics reveal that 65 percent of us will at some time require supervised care by a medical professional either at home, in a nursing home, or in an assisted care living facility.
- Conventional long term care insurance can be expensive but less so if purchased when you are young, and like any life insurance product, it can provide you with peace of mind.
- Some annuities and newer life insurance policies that specify a Living Benefit can provide the insured with a stipend each month to help defray the costs of long term care. The benefit of a life insurance policy with a Living Benefit is that the policy will pay your beneficiaries when you die as well as paying you while you are still alive to help fund long term care.
- If you or your spouse is a war veteran, you may qualify for the Aid and Attendance. This benefit is designed to assist a veteran or spouse paying out of pocket for long term care and is available to individuals who reside in assisted living communities, personal care homes, skilled nursing facilities and those receiving personal in-home care.

3

FUELING YOUR ENTERPRISE

*"I'm sorry, Commander, but I've learned we can't afford to die here—
not even once."*
                              – Dr. Julian Bashir, Star Trek: Deep Space Nine

Death to your retirement enterprise means running out of money.
As Dr. Bashir notes, dying even one time is an unacceptable option, which is why evaluating your income needs lies at the heart
of retirement planning. Finding the most efficient and beneficial
way to address these income needs affects not just your everyday
reality, but the ability of your money to provide for you throughout the length of your retirement journey.

> » *Katherine retired young at the age of 53. Because she feared
> outliving her money, Katherine went to see a financial profes-
> sional who could help her protect her lifestyle. She told him*

her goals were to have good income with some growth, because she wanted to leave a legacy for her daughter and granddaughter. Katherine also wanted to protect herself from the high cost of long term care. Longevity ran in her family—her grandmother had lived to be 95 years old—so Katherine was looking at income needs that could last as long as 40 years.

After understanding her needs, the financial professional secured a portion of Katherine's portfolio in a safe, Green Money investment that would generate the income she needed to live on for the first 10 years. He also helped her to maximize her Social Security benefit so that when she turned 70 and triggered the benefit, it would provide for 60 percent of her income needs. He also set up five other investments—or buckets of money—designed for growth. These buckets were in Light Green, Dark Green and Yellow Money investments. These additional buckets of money gave Katherine growth and the ability to increase her income down the road, countering the effects of inflation, potential tax increases or health care needs that could stress her lifestyle.

INCOME PLANNING IN THE BAG

Remember those Big Audacious Goals? Retirement planning is about more than just making ends meet. It's about your goals, your dreams and the experiences you want to have. The money you have so carefully put away can be used to help attain those goals and live out those dreams if you take a planful approach. This is where your Green Money comes into play: the safer, more reliable assets that you have accumulated which are designed to provide you with a steady income. On day one of your retirement, you will need a steady and reliable supply of income from your Green Money.

Take a moment to think about your income goals:

- What is your lifestyle today?

- Would you like to maintain it into retirement?
- Are you meeting your needs?
- Are you happy with your lifestyle?
- What do you really *need* to live on when you retire?

While the income amount will be different for everyone, the general rule of thumb is that a retiree will require 70 to 80 percent of their pre-retirement income to maintain their lifestyle. Arriving at a realistic number might require a conversation with your financial professional.

> » *Sulu sits down with his financial professional to figure out a realistic retirement budget. After going through the bills, his financial professional asks,*
> *"Do you have a car payment?"*
> *"No," Sulu replies. "We own a car."*
> *"Okay. When you bought your car, what did you buy?"*
> *"We bought a used Toyota Camry. Before that, we had a Camry that lasted us about eight years. When it got up to 80,000 miles we traded it in for another because after that, things start to go wrong, and I don't want to have to worry about repairs. I like to take road trips to visit my kids."*
> *"Okay, then let's budget for that. If you buy a new Camry for $30,000 and receive about $10,000 for a trade-in amount, we'll want to budget for an additional $20,000 every eight years. That's about $2,500 to $3,000 a year we have to put aside someplace to budget the purchase of a new car."*
> *By planning ahead for this expense, Sulu is able to achieve his goal of a new car every eight years while saving money in taxes and keeping his lifestyle intact.*

HOW TO FACTOR INFLATION

Once you have identified your annual expenses, the key becomes matching your income need with the correct investment strategies, options and tools to satisfy that need. You want to know how much to structure for income now and how much to be set in Light or Dark Green buckets for later growth. As taxes increase and inflation erodes away at your buying power, you may find that your income needs actually increase over the course of your retirement years. It might cost more to buy a new car 10 years from now than it does today. When you are on a fixed income, how do you combat the fluctuating prices of food, fuel and healthcare? A hundred dollars today won't be the same hundred dollars a few light years from now.

Since 1975, the Social Security administration has been conducting annual cost-of-living adjustments (COLA) to ensure that the purchasing power of its benefits is not eroded by inflation.* The amount of the COLA increase is measured by the Consumer Price Index for Urban Wage Earners and Clerical Workers (CPI-W) as prepared by the Bureau of Labor Statistics.** When you are living on a fixed income, the rising cost of basic human essentials means that your quality of living can, over time, go down. A good income plan takes these price fluctuations into account.

You want your income stream to have an element of COLA built in, so that as you age, your income sees an increase in proportion to today's economic environment of rising prices.

One way to create an income plan with a built-in cost of living adjustment is through a growth component of your investment strategy. Some items on your expense list don't need to be adjusted for COLA—such as a fixed mortgage payment. Other items, such as new vehicles, will require planning. As we determined earlier

---

* http://www.ssa.gov/OACT/COLA/colasummary.html
** http://www.socialsecurity.gov/news/cola/2014/factsheet.htm

in Chapters One and Two, the most important thing you need to do as you create an income plan is to protect your principal and avoid too much exposure to risk. Combining this strategy with a growth component will secure your income needs for down the road.

WHAT IF YOU NEED TO REFUEL?

Just as there is a lot of space out there between the stars, your retirement is also a long journey. What if one spouse dies—how will you replace that pension? How will you replace their Social Security?

There are many investment tools designed to provide spousal continuation, such as life insurance policies that provide for tax-free income and newer indexed products that offer a joint life option so both spouses are protected against income loss. Still other couples choose to set aside a separate bucket of money in a Dark Green or Light Green investment that is allowed to grow. This income stream isn't turned on until the money is needed. With Green Money investments, you have control over when to turn on or off the income stream. You could use this money to replace income or to fund the replacement of a roof—the choice is yours.

Avoiding poverty as a retired widow means taking into consideration what your financial picture would look like if one spouse passes away. Ideally, both spouses should be involved in the income planning process. If your husband or wife handles all the accounts, make sure you understand how much income will be coming if he or she passes away. Also find out whether or not that income comes from a guaranteed source.

The first place we look for income producing sources are Safe Money options such as pensions and Social Security. The amount of income provided by those sources can't be changed, and they provide the retirement base that you build up from until you reach the number you need. A financial professional can help you customize an income plan based on your retirement goals and current expenses by utilizing a strategy that provides for both growth and opportunity to meet your short and long term income requirements.

CHAPTER 3 RECAP //

- The foundation of a retirement strategy depends on knowing how much money you need, when you need it and who you need it to provide for.
- Having a growth component of your income plan is crucial to today's retirees who are living longer and enjoying more retirement years than their parents. Adjusting for inflation means structuring your investments so they allow for an increase in income needs in five, 10 or 20 years. Using Light or Dark Green investments is one way to achieve durability of income.
- Spousal continuation is one area often overlooked by retirees. When one spouse dies, the loss of pensions and monetary benefits such as Social Security means a reduction in monthly income. Your income plan should take into consideration guaranteed sources of income that will still be available after your spouse passes away.

THE TROUBLE WITH TRIBBLES: UNDERSTANDING SOCIAL SECURITY OPTIONS

"Just before they went into warp, I beamed the whole kit and kaboodle into their engine room, where they'll be no tribble at all."
— *Scotty, Star Trek: The Original Series*

The trouble with Social Security is that the majority of Americans—74 percent to be exact—receive reduced benefits because they file at the wrong time.* Like lemmings jumping over a cliff, they follow the herd without realizing how adversely this decision

---

When to Claim Social Security Benefits, David Blanchett, CFA, CFP January, 2013*

can affect your financial future. There are over 4,000 options for a married couple filing for Social Security today. All these options can turn the warm fuzzy feeling that a benefit should give you into a burgeoning problem.

» *Deanna starting taking her Social Security benefit at the age of 62 because she was laid off from her job at the age of 61. She began receiving her Social Security checks for $800 a month and continued to look for another job. Her husband also triggered his Social Security benefit. A few months after turning 62, Deanna found a pretty good job working for a medical clinic. This employment paid her over $20,000 annually, and Deanna got busy. She didn't turn off her Social Security benefit because she didn't know that she could. The trouble this caused Deanna was twofold:*

First, because she started her benefit at her earliest retirement age, she was penalized 25 percent, and this penalty was locked in after the first year. That meant Deanna would continue receiving 25 percent less money every month for the rest of her life.

Second, because she was working while receiving her Social Security benefit, Deanna was penalized again. As of 2014, the penalty for working while receiving your benefit will cost you $1 for every $2 dollars earned over the amount of $15,480.*

When Deanna found out about this penalty, she made an appointment to talk to a financial professional who could run her a Social Security optimization report. She found out that once you start claiming your benefit, you do have the option of changing your mind if you act before the first 12 months are over and pay back all the benefits received. Unfortunately

---

* *http://www.ssa.gov/retire2/whileworking.htm*

for Deanna, she waited one month too long to find this out, and the deadline for changing her filing options had passed. Had she maximized her benefit and filed differently, Deanna would have received $100,000 more income during her lifetime.

While Deanna will be able to receive her $800 a month once she stops working, she will never be able to get the amount she was entitled to at Full Retirement Age. Social Security turned into trouble for Deanna due to lack of knowledge. For most people, working while claiming Social Security is a bad idea. Unless you have health considerations or are really in a financial pinch, it doesn't make a whole lot of sense to be paying out $1 for every $2 that you earn.

These penalties and other early withdrawal charges are designed by the Social Security administration to encourage retirees to keep working a little longer. For Boomers who enjoy their job, this can be a positive thing, and an opportunity to let your Social Security benefit grow for later. The longer you work, the more money is paid into the system, and there are many other options and filing strategies, especially for married couples, that can significantly increase your monthly and lifetime benefit. Whether or not these strategies will benefit you depends on your individual situation. Learning how to apply these options can help you get the most out of this important monthly benefit.

CLAIM SOME NOW AND CLAIM MORE LATER

The Retired Worker Benefit is what most people are talking about when they refer to Social Security. This is your benefit based on your earnings and the amount that you have paid into the system over the span of your career. There are five other benefits that most people aren't as familiar with that are especially important for married couples. Learning how these benefits can maximize your lifetime income just might give you a way to claim some money *now* while allowing your benefit to grow, or roll-up, so you can *claim even more money later.*

File and Suspend: This concept allows you to file at age 66 (which is Full Retirement Age or FRA) and suspend the benefit. This means your benefit amount will continue to roll up, or grow each year at a rate of 8 percent. Once you file and suspend, you can trigger the benefit any time you want, but after age 70, the benefit no longer grows.

You don't have to be a married individual in order to file and suspend. Filing and then waiting to claim your benefit allows you to receive a higher lifetime benefit, and should an unexpected health issue develop, you are able to go backwards in time and claim your benefit retroactively from the date of the original filing. This is a little-known rule which can result in thousands more for you, your spouse and your legacy, which is why meeting with a financial professional educated about the finer points of Social Security can really be worth your time.

Restricted Application: A higher-earning spouse is able to start collecting a portion of the lower-earning spousal benefit (claim some now) while allowing his or her benefit to continue to grow (claim more later!)

For example, Deanna in our story above had a spouse who was eligible to receive $3,000 a month if he waited until age 70. He filed early because they needed the additional income, but what he could have done was filed a restricted application. This would have given him half of Deanna's retirement benefit every month while still allowing his own benefit to grow. Because he wasn't working, the half he earned would not have been penalized, and the couple would have received more money. This strategy would have also increased their overall lifetime family benefit because once he turned 70, he would have received that $3,000 a month for the rest of his life. Be clear when you file that you are restricting the application to the spousal benefit only, and not collecting your own benefit.

Spousal Benefit: The Spousal Benefit is a good option when one spouse's benefit is significantly lower than the other's. This benefit can work in tandem with File and Suspend. The lower-earning spouse is eligible to receive up to 50 percent of the higher-earning spouse's benefit without triggering their own benefit. For example, if your wife is eligible to receive $2,000 a month, and your benefit is only $500 a month, you can File and Suspend and then claim the Spousal Benefit. Your own benefit continues to grow at the 8 percent rate. At the same time, you will receive 50 percent of your spouse's benefit, which in this case amounts to an extra check for $1,000 a month.

Divorced Spouse: If you have gone through a divorce and were married for at least 10 years, you might be eligible to receive 50 percent of your former spouse's benefit. There are a few qualifications that must be met before you can receive this benefit:
- You were married to your former spouse for at least 10 years.
- You are at least 62 years old.
- You are currently single and thus not eligible for the Spousal Benefits mentioned above.
- You aren't entitled to a higher Social Security benefit on your own record.*

Survivor Benefit: This benefit allows the surviving spouse to receive the higher of the two benefits in the event of death. For

---

* *http://www.ssa.gov/retire2/yourdivspouse.htm*

example, if your wife is eligible to receive $3,000 a month and your benefit is only $1,000 a month, your income would drop significantly should your wife pass away. The Survivor Benefit dictates that in the event of her death, you could elect the higher of the two benefits. Instead of only receiving $1,000 a month, you would receive $3,000. Many widows don't know about this benefit and are living near or in poverty due to lack of knowledge.

WHERE SHOULD YOU GO TO FOR ADVICE?

Social Security is a guaranteed, Green Money source of income that is an important part of the big picture when it comes to the longevity of your income during retirement. Social Security employees can give you information, but they are banned from providing advice and recommendations about how you can maximize your individual situation. If you want a truly accurate understanding of when and how to file, you need someone who will ask you the right questions about your situation, someone who has access to specialized software that can crunch the numbers. The reality is that you need to work with a professional that can provide you with the sophisticated analysis of your situation that will help you make a truly informed decision.

Ideally, you want to work with a financial professional who can run a Social Security Maximization Report. The Social Security Maximization Report is not a product we sell but a service that we offer. The report generates an individualized understanding of how and when to file for your Social Security to get the most out of this important benefit. When you get your customized Social Security Maximization Report, you will not only know all the options available to you—but you will understand the financial implications of each choice. In addition to the analysis, you will also get a report that shows *exactly* at what age—including which month and year—you should trigger benefits and how you should apply. It also includes a variety of other time-specific recommendations, such as when to apply for Medicare or take Required Minimum Distributions from your qualified plans. A report means there is no need to wonder, or to try to figure out when to take action—the Social Security Maximization Report lays it all out for you in plain English.

A CRASH COURSE IN SOCIAL SECURITY

Here are some facts that illustrate how Americans currently use Social Security:

- 90 percent of Americans age 65 and older receive Social Security benefits.*
- Social Security provides 39 percent of income for retired Americans.*
- Claiming Social Security benefits at the wrong time can reduce your monthly benefit by up to 57 percent.**
- 43 percent of men and 48 percent of women claim Social Security benefits at age 62.**
- 74 percent of retirees receive reduced Social Security benefits.**
- In 2013, the average monthly Social Security benefit was $1,261. *The maximum benefit for 2013 was $2,533. The $1,272 monthly benefit reduction between the average and the maximum is applied for life.* ***

There are many aspects of Social Security that are well known and others that aren't. Social Security is a massive government program that manages retirement benefits for millions of people. Experts spend their entire careers understanding and analyzing it. Luckily, you don't have to understand all of the intricacies of So-

---

* *http://www.ssa.gov/pressoffice/basicfact.htm*
** *When to Claim Social Security Benefits, David Blanchett, CFA, CFP® January, 2013*
*** *http://www.socialsecurity.gov/pressoffice/factsheets/colafacts2013.com*

cial Security to maximize its advantages. You simply need to know the best way to manage your Social Security benefit. You need to know exactly what to do to get the most from your Social Security benefit and when to do it. Taking the time to create a roadmap for your Social Security strategy will help ensure that you are able to exact your maximum benefit and efficiently coordinate it with the rest of your retirement plan.

There are many aspects of Social Security that you have no control over. You don't control how much you put into it, and you don't control what it's invested in or how the government manages it. **However, you do control when and how you file for benefits.** The real question about Social Security that you need to answer is, "When should I start taking Social Security?" While this is the all-important question, there are a couple of key pieces of information you need to track down first. Before we get into the calculations and strategies, let's start by covering the basic information about Social Security which should give you an idea of where you stand.

Eligibility. Understanding how and when you are eligible for Social Security benefits will help clarify what to expect when the time comes to claim them.

To receive retirement benefits from Social Security, you must earn eligibility. In almost all cases, Americans born after 1929 must earn 40 quarters of credit to be eligible to draw their Social Security retirement benefit. In 2013, a Social Security credit represented $1,160 earned in a calendar quarter. The number changes as it is indexed each year, but not drastically. In 2012, a credit represented $1,130. Four quarters of credit is the maximum number that can be earned each year. In 2013, an American would have had to earn at least $4,640 to accumulate four credits. In order to qualify for retirement benefits, you must have earned a minimum number of credits. Additionally, if you are at least 62 years old and have been married to a recipient of Social Security benefits for at least 12 months, you can choose to receive Spousal Benefits. Although 40 is the minimum number of credits required to begin drawing benefits, it is important to know that once you claim your Social Security benefit, there is no going back. Although there may be cost of living adjustments made, you are locked into that base benefit amount forever.

Primary Insurance Amount. You can think of your Primary Insurance Amount (PIA) like a ripening fruit. It represents the amount of your Social Security benefit at your Full Retirement Age (FRA). Your benefit becomes fully ripe at your FRA, and will neither reduce nor increase due to early or delayed retirement options. If you opt to take benefits before your FRA, however, your monthly benefit will be less than your PIA. You will essentially be picking an unripened fruit. On the one hand, waiting until after your FRA to access your benefits will increase your benefit beyond your PIA. On the other hand, you don't want the fruit to overripen, because every month you wait is one less check you get from the government.

Full Retirement Age. Your FRA is an important figure for anyone who is planning to rely on Social Security benefits in their retirement. Depending on when you were born, there is a specific age at which you will attain FRA. Your FRA is dictated by your year of birth and is the age at which you can begin your full monthly benefit. Your FRA is important because it is half of the equation used to calculate your Social Security benefit. The other half of the equation is based on when you start taking benefits.

When Social Security was initially set up, the FRA was age 65, and it still is for people born before 1938. But as time has passed, the age for receiving full retirement benefits has increased. If you were born between 1938 and 1960, your full retirement age is somewhere on a sliding scale between 65 and 67. Anyone born in 1960 or later will now have to wait until age 67 for full benefits. Increasing the FRA has helped the government reduce the cost of the Social Security program, which pays out more than a half trillion dollars to beneficiaries every year!*

While you can begin collecting benefits as early as age 62, the amount you receive as a monthly benefit will be less than it would be if you wait until you reached your FRA or surpass your FRA. It is important to note that if you file for Social Security benefit before your FRA, *the reduction to your monthly benefit will remain in place for the rest of your life.* You can also delay receiving benefits up to age 70, in which case your benefits will be higher than your PIA for the rest of your life.

- At FRA, 100 percent of PIA is available as a monthly benefit.
- At age 62, your Social Security retirement benefits are available. For each month you take benefits prior to your FRA, however, the monthly amount of your benefit is reduced. *This reduction stays in place for the rest of your life.*
- At age 70, your monthly benefit reaches its maximum. After you turn age 70, your monthly benefit will no longer increase.

Year of Birth	Full Retirement Age
1943-1954	66
1955	66 and 2 months
1956	66 and 4 months
1957	66 and 6 months
1958	66 and 8 months
1959	66 and 10 months
1960 or later	age 67**

---

* http://www.ssa.gov/pressoffice/basicfact.htm
** http://www.ssa.gov/OACT/progdata/nra.html

ROLLING UP YOUR SOCIAL SECURITY

Your Social Security income "rolls up" the longer you wait to claim it. Your monthly benefit will continue to increase until you turn 70 years old. But because Social Security is the foundation of most people's retirement, many Americans feel that they don't have control over how or when they receive their benefits. As a matter of fact, only 4 percent of Americans wait until after their FRA to file for benefits! This trend persists, despite the fact that every dollar you increase your Social Security income by means less money you will have to spend from your nest egg to meet your retirement income needs! For many people, creating their Social Security strategy is the most important decision they can make to positively impact their retirement. *The difference between the best and worst Social Security decision can be tens of thousands of dollars over a lifetime of benefits—up to $170,000!*

Deciding NOW or LATER: Following the above logic, it makes sense to wait as long as you can to begin receiving your Social Security benefit. However, the answer isn't always that simple. Not everyone has the option of waiting. Many people need to rely on Social Security on day one of their retirement. In fact, *nearly 50 percent of 62-year-old Americans file for Social Security benefits.* Why is this number so high? Some might need the income. Others might be in poor health and don't feel they will live long enough to make FRA worthwhile for themselves or their families. It is also possible, however, that the majority of folks taking an early benefit at age 62 are simply under-informed about Social Security. Perhaps they make this major decision based on rumors and emotion.

File Immediately if You:
- Find your job is unbearable.
- Are willing to sacrifice retirement income.
- Are not healthy and need a reliable source of income.

Consider Delaying Your Benefit if You:
- Want to maximize your retirement income.
- Want to increase retirement benefits for your spouse.
- Are still working and like it.
- Are healthy and willing / able to wait to file.

So if you decide to wait, how long should you wait? Lots of people can put it off for a few years, but not everyone can wait until they are 70 years old. Your individual circumstances may be able to help you determine when you should begin taking Social Security. If you do the math, you will quickly see that between ages 62 and 70, there are 96 months in which you can file for your Social Security benefit. If you take into account those 96 months and the 96 months your spouse could also file for Social Security, the number of different strategies for structuring your benefit, you can easily end up with more than 20,000 different scenarios. It's safe to say this isn't the kind of math that most people can easily handle. Each month would result in a different benefit amount. The longer you wait, the higher your monthly benefit amount becomes. Each month you wait, however, is one less month that you receive a Social Security check.

The goal is to maximize your lifetime benefits. That may not always mean waiting until you can get the largest monthly payment. Taking the bigger picture into account, you want to find out how to get the most money out of Social Security over the number of years that you draw from it. Don't underestimate the power of optimizing your benefit: the difference between the BEST and WORST Social Security election can easily be between $30,000 to $50,000 in lifetime benefits. ***The difference can be very substantial!***

If you know that every month you wait, your Social Security benefit goes up a little bit, and you also know that every month you wait, you receive one less benefit check, how do you determine where the sweet spot is that maximizes your benefits over your lifetime? Financial professionals have access to software that will calculate the best year and month for you to file for benefits based on your default life expectancy. You can further customize that information by estimating your life expectancy based on your health, habits and family history. If you can then create an income plan (we'll get into this later in the chapter) that helps you wait until the target date for you to file for Social Security, you can optimize your retirement income strategy to get the most out of your Social Security benefit. How can you calculate your life expectancy? Well, you don't know exactly how long you'll live, but you have a better idea than the government does. They rely on averages to make their calculations. *You have much more personal information about your health, lifestyle and family history than they do.* You can use that knowledge to game the system and beat all the other people who are making uninformed decisions by filing early for Social Security.

While you can and should educate yourself about how Social Security works, the reality is you don't need to know a lot of general information about Social Security in order to make choices about your retirement. What you do need to know is exactly *what to do to maximize your benefit.* Because knowing what you need to do has huge impacts on your retirement! For most Americans, Social Security is the foundation of income planning for retirement. Social Security benefits represent nearly 40 percent of the income of retirees.* For many people, it can represent the largest portion of their retirement income. Not treating your Social Security benefit as an asset and investment tool can lead to sub-optimization of your largest source of retirement income.

Let's take a look at an example that shows the impact of working with a financial professional to optimize Social Security benefits:

---

* *http://www.socialsecurity.gov/pressoffice/basicfact.htm*

» *Lucas and Jean Picard are a typical American couple who have worked their whole lives and saved when they could. Lucas is 60 years old, and Jean is 56 years old. They sat down with a financial professional who logged onto the Social Security website to look up their PIAs. Lucas's PIA is $1,900 and Jean's is $900.*

If the Picards cash in at age 62 and begin taking retirement benefits from Social Security, they will receive an estimated $492,000 in lifetime benefits. That may seem like a lot, but if you divide that amount over 20 years, it averages out to be just shy of $25,000 per year. The Picards are accustomed to a more significant annual income than that. To make up the difference, they will have to rely on alternative retirement income options. They will basically have to depend on a bigger nest egg to provide them with the income they need.

If they wait until their FRA, they will increase their lifetime benefits to an estimated $523,700. This option allows them to achieve their Primary Insurance Amount, which will provide them a $33,000 annual income.

After learning the Picards' needs and using software to calculate the most optimal time to begin drawing benefits, the Picards' financial professional determined that the best option for them drastically increases their potential lifetime benefits to $660,000!

*By using strategies that their financial professional recommended, they increased their potential lifetime benefits by as much as **$148,000.** There's no telling how much you could miss out on from your Social Security if you don't take time to create a strategy that calculates your maximum benefit. For the Picards, the value of maximizing their benefits was the difference between night and day. While this may seem like a special case, it isn't uncommon to find benefit increases of this* *magnitude. You'll never know unless you take a look at your own options.*

Despite the importance of knowing when and how to take your Social Security benefit, many of today's retirees and pre-retirees may know little about the mechanics of Social Security and how they can maximize their benefit.

MAXIMIZING YOUR LIFETIME BENEFIT

As discussed in Chapter 2, calculating how to maximize **lifetime benefits** is more important than waiting until age 70 for your maximum **monthly benefit amount.** It's about getting the most income during your lifetime. Professional benefit maximization software can target the year and month that it is most beneficial for you to file based on your life expectancy.

The three most common ages that people associate with retirement benefits are 62 (Earliest Eligible Age), 66 (Full Retirement Age), and 70 (age at which monthly maximum benefit is reached). In almost all circumstances, however, none of those three most common ages will give you the maximum lifetime benefit.

Remember, every month you wait to file, the amount of your benefit check goes up, but you also get one less check. With all of the different options, strategies and benefits to choose from, you can see why filing for Social Security is more complicated than just mailing in the paperwork. Gathering the data and making yourself aware of all your different options isn't enough to know exactly what to do, however. On the one hand, you can knock yourself out trying to figure out which options are best for you and wondering if you made the best decision. On the other hand, you can work with a financial professional who uses customized software that takes all the variables of your specific situation into account and calculates your best option.

You have tens of thousands of different options for filing for your Social Security benefit. You don't know exactly how long you're going to live, but you have a better idea of your life expectancy than the actuaries at the Social Security Administration who can only work with averages. They can't make calculations based on your specific situation. A professional can run the numbers for you and get the target date that maximizes your potential lifetime benefits. You can't get this information from the SSA, but you *can* get it from a financial professional.

Review Questions about Your Social Security Benefit:
- How can I maximize my lifetime benefit? By knowing when and how to file for Social Security. This usually means waiting until you have at least reached your Full Retirement Age. A professional has the experience and the tools to help determine when and how you can maximize your lifetime benefits.
- Who will provide reliable advice for making these decisions? Only a professional has the tools and experience to provide you reliable advice.
- Will the Social Security Administration provide me with the advice? The Social Security Administration cannot provide you with advice or strategies for claiming your benefit. They can give you information about your monthly benefit, but that's it. They also don't have the tools to tell you what your specific best option is. They can accurately answer how the system works, but they can't advise you on what decision to make as to how and when to file for benefits

CHAPTER 4 RECAP //

- Working while taking your Social Security benefit causes you to be penalized $1 for every $2 you make over $15,480 as of 2014. Claiming your Social Security at age 62 also reduces your benefit by 25 percent.

- If you change your mind about when you wish to receive your Social Security benefit, you have the option to cancel as long as you do it within the first year of receiving benefits and pay back the full dollar amount of all benefits received.

- There are several important benefits for married couples that can provide additional income. These benefits include the following: Restricted Application, File and Suspend, Spousal Benefit, Divorced Spouse benefit, and the Survivor Benefit.

- You cannot get advice about how to maximize your lifetime benefit from a Social Security representative. They are prohibited from giving advice about when to elect your benefit options.

- To get the most out of your Social Security benefit, you need to file at the right time. Every dollar your Social Security income increases is less money you'll have to spend from your retirement savings to supplement your income. A financial professional can help you determine when you should file for Social Security to get your Maximum Lifetime Benefit.

- Deciding when to take your Social Security benefit is one of the most important decisions you make as a retiree. After the first year of taking the benefit, that amount is locked in for the duration of your lifetime.

5

FILLING THE VOID:
WHAT IF SOCIAL SECURITY ISN'T ENOUGH?

"I do not smirk—but if I did, this would be a good opportunity."
                                        —*Worf, Star Trek: Deep Space Nine*

The moment that you stop working and start living off the money that you've set aside for retirement can be compared to stepping out into the void. You've worked and earned money your whole life, but the day that you retire, that income comes to an end. That's the day that you have to rely on your other assets that fill the void. You may have a pension, an IRA or Roth IRA, dividends from stock holdings, money from the sale of real estate, rental property, or other sources of income. Social Security might also fill more of the void than you think, especially if you take steps to maximize your benefit, but even then you will likely have several income gaps to fill.

Income gaps represent the difference between the income you have and the income need. Most Boomers find it in their best interest to plan ahead for the likelihood of more than one income gap:

- **Gap #1**: The difference between your known guaranteed sources of income and your lifestyle needs.
- **Gap #2**: The gap that could be present when using Social Security claiming strategies such as File and Suspend. This is usually a 3 to 8 year gap that can easily be filled using Dark Green or Light Green Money investments.
- **Gap #3**: Spousal continuation and long term care needs. This is a gap that we usually plan for after the age of 70.

The good news is that there are several financial products designed specifically to fill these income gaps, and all of them are Green Money investment opportunities, which is reason enough to smile (or smirk, as the case may be.)

TAKING A HYBRID APPROACH TO YOUR INCOME NEEDS

You looked at Social Security strategies earlier, discovering you have some control over how and when you file. Those decisions can change the outcome of your benefit in your favor. Once you start drawing that income, it is safer and will provide you with a reliable source of income for the rest of your life. While there are many factors of Social Security that you can control, there are many that you cannot.

For example, you do not have the choice of putting more money into Social Security in order to get more out of it. If you could have the option to contribute more money toward Social Security in order to secure a guaranteed income, it would be a great way to create a Green Money asset that would enhance your retirement. Since that option isn't available, you may seek an investment tool that is similar to Social Security that provides you with a reliable income. It also has the potential to increase the value of your principal investment! This kind of win-win situation exists, and it's called an annuity.

Today, you probably have savings in a variety of assets that you acquired over the years. But you may not have taken time to examine them and assess how they will support your retirement. **As discussed earlier, it's not about whether the market goes up or down, but when it does.** If it goes down during the early years of your retirement, you could be in serious danger of outliving your income. If outliving your money is of concern to you, an annuity may be a good choice.

In the last 20 years since indexed annuities were created, they have actually become their own asset class. They were designed to offer attractive returns somewhere between bonds and equities, but with zero the risk. Indexed annuities purchased with income riders can offer the perfect marriage of risk and return. During short bursts of five to 10 years, they can actually outperform basic markets like the S&P 500, because when the markets drop by 20 percent or even 40 percent, indexed annuities have no downside. They can't lose money, and your previous gains are locked in. What this means for the investor is that during good times you can capture the upside of the market without the downside risk. You can lock in your gains every year while accessing income benefits that can be turned on to fill the income gaps just when you need the money. If you're fortunate enough to live into your 100s, an income rider can guarantee that you'll always have the income you need for long as you live, thus solving the problem of longevity. Annuities also offer increased or higher death benefits if that is important to you.

Ask yourself the following questions:

- How concerned are you about finding a secure financial vehicle to protect your savings?
- How concerned are you that there may be a better way to structure your savings?

If you are concerned about the best way to fill your income gap, an income annuity investment tool is likely a good option for you. Income annuities have many similar qualities to Social Security that give them the same look and feel as that reliable benefit check you get every month. Most importantly, an income annuity can be an efficient and profitable way to solve your income gaps.

HOW ANNUITIES FIT INTO AN OVERALL INCOME PLAN

Annuities are popular and reliable investment tools that allow you to secure income during retirement. In its simplest form, an annuity is a way to invest your money that allows you to structure it for income. Annuities come in a variety of modes. Finding the right one for you will take a conversation with your financial professional. Be sure you fully understand the features, benefits and costs of any annuity you are considering before investing money. The following example shows just how helpful an indexed annuity option can be for a retiree:

> » *Leonard and Eleanor McCoy are 62 years old and have decided to run the numbers to see what their retirement is going to look like. They know they currently need $6,000 per month to pay their bills and maintain their current lifestyle. They have also done their Social Security homework and have determined that, between the two of them, they will receive $4,200 per month in benefits. They also receive $350 per month in rent from a tenant who lives in a small carriage*

house in their backyard. Between their Social Security and the monthly rent income, they will be short $1,450 per month. They do have an additional asset, however. They have been contributing for years to an IRA that has reached a value of $350,000. They realize that they have to figure out how to turn the $350,000 in their IRA into $1,450 per month for the rest of their life. At first glance, it may seem like they will have plenty of money. With some quick calculations, they find they have 240 months, or nearly 20 years, of monthly income before they exhaust the account. When you consider income tax, the potential for higher taxes in the future, and market fluctuations (because many IRAs are invested in the market), the amount in the IRA seems to have a little less clout. Every dollar the McCoys take out of the IRA is subject to income tax, and if they leave the remainder in the IRA, they run the risk of losing money in a volatile market. Once they retire and stop getting a paycheck every two weeks, they also stop con-tributing to their IRA. And when they aren't supplementing its growth with their own money, they are entirely dependent on market growth. That's a scary prospect. They could also withdraw the money from the IRA and put it in a savings account or CD, but removing all the money at once will put them in a tax bracket that will claim a huge portion of the value of the IRA. A seemingly straightforward asset has now become a complicated equation. The McCoys didn't know what to do, so they met with their financial professional.

Their financial professional suggested that they use the money to purchase an indexed annuity with an income rider. They selected an annuity that was designed for their specific situation. They took the lump sum from their IRA, placed it in an indexed annuity taking advantage of annual reset so they never lost the value of their investment. In return, they were guaranteed the $1,450 of income per month that they *needed to meet their retirement goals. The simplicity of the contract allowed them to do an analysis with their professional just once to understand the product. They basically put their money in an investment crockpot where they didn't have to look at it or manage it. They just needed to let it simmer. In fact, their professional was able to find an annuity for them that allowed them their $1,450 monthly payment with a lump sum of $249,455, leaving them more than $100,000 to reinvest somewhere else. Keep in mind that annuities are tax deferred, meaning you will pay tax on the income you receive from an annuity in the year you receive it.*

HOW INCOME ANNUITIES WORK

When you put your money into an annuity, you are essentially buying an investment product from an insurance company. It is a contract between you and the insurance company that provides the investment tool. Let's say you have saved $100,000 and need it to generate income to meet your needs above and beyond your Social Security and pension checks. You give the $100,000 to an insurance company, who in turn invests it to generate growth.

They usually select investments that have modest returns over long term horizons. In other words, they generally put it somewhere stable and predictable. Most commonly, they will invest it in a combination of bonds and treasuries that are safer and dependable ways to grow money. They use the money from the insurance products they sell to invest, use a portion of the returns to generate profits for themselves, and return a portion to clients in the form of payouts, claims, and structured income options.

One of the most attractive qualities of these types of annuities is something called annual reset. Annual reset is sometimes also referred to as a "ratcheting." Instead of taking on the risk that comes with putting money in a fluctuating market, you can offset that risk onto the insurance company. It works like this: If the market goes down, you don't suffer a loss. Instead, the insurance company absorbs it. But if the market goes up, you share with the insurance company some of the profit made on the gain. The amount of gain you get is called your annuity participation rate. Typically the insurer will cap the amount of gain you can realize at somewhere between 3 and 7 percent. If the market goes up 10 percent, you would realize a portion of that gain (whatever percentage you are capped at). This means you to never lose money on your investment, while always gaining a portion of the upswings. The measurement period of your annuity can be calculated monthly, weekly and even daily, but most annuities are measured annually. The level of the index when you buy and the index level one year later will determine the amount of loss or gain. You and the insurance company are betting that the market will generally go up over time.

The graph below shows how the power of annual reset can work to protect your principal. The top line reflects the Income Rider Value of an account with an income rider attached. The value of this account can never drop, but you are never able to access this money except through regular income payments. There is also a fee for an income rider. The middle line, Accumulation Value, reflects the actual account value. This is money that you can access and this account can be emptied. If you elect to purchase an income rider and the actual account value drops to zero, you are still guaranteed your monthly income payments because FIAs purchased with income riders guarantee an income stream for life. The red line shows the performance of the S&P 500 over the same period of time.

WHAT IS AN INCOME RIDER?

When you use that $100,000 to buy a contract with an insurance company in the form of an annuity, you are pegging your money on an index. It could be the S&P 500, the Dow Jones Industrial

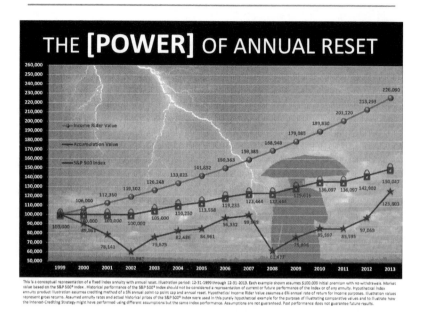

THE [POWER] OF ANNUAL RESET

This is a conceptual representation of a fixed index annuity with annual reset. Illustration period: 12-31-1999 through 12-31-2013. Each example shown assumes $100,000 initial premium with no withdrawals. Market value based on the S&P 500® index . Historical performance of the S&P 500® Index should not be considered a representation of current or future performance of the Index or of any annuity. Hypothetical Index annuity product illustration assumes crediting method of a 5% annual point-to point cap and annual reset. Hypothetical Income Rider Value assumes a 6% annual rate of return for income purposes. Illustration values represent gross returns. Assumed annuity rates and actual historical prices of the S&P 500® Index were used in this purely hypothetical example for the purpose of illustrating comparative values and to illustrate how the Interest-Crediting Strategy might have performed using different assumptions but the same Index performance. Assumptions are not guaranteed. Past performance does not guarantee future results.

Average or any number of indexes. To generate income from the annuity, you select something called an income rider. An income rider is a subset of an indexed annuity. Essentially, it is the amount of money from which the insurance company will pay you an income while you have your money in their annuity. Your income rider is a larger number than what your investment is actually worth, and if you select the income rider, it will increase in value over time, providing you with more income. As the insurance company holds your money and invests it, they generate a return on it that they use to pay you a regular monthly income based on a higher number. The insurance company has to outperform the amount that they pay you in order to make a profit.

Remember, insurance companies make long-term investments that provide them with predictable flows of money. They like to stabilize the amount of money that goes in and out of their doors instead of paying and receiving large unpredictable chunks at once. When you opt for an income rider, an insurance company can reliably predict how much money they will pay out to you over a set period of time. It's predictable, and they like that. They can base their business on those predictable numbers.

In order to encourage investors to leave their money in their annuity contracts, insurance companies create surrender periods that protect their investments. If you remove your money from the annuity contract during the surrender period, you will pay a penalty and will not be able to receive your entire investment amount back. A typical surrender period is 10 years. If after three years you decide that you want your $100,000 back, the insurance company has that money tied up in bonds and other investments with the understanding that they will have it for another seven years. Because they will take a hit on removing the money from

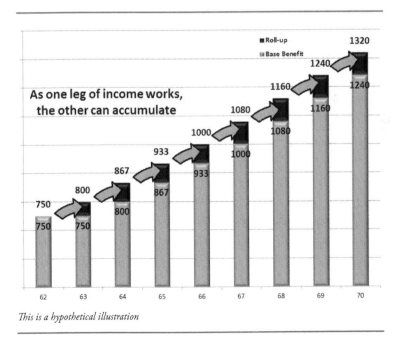

This is a hypothetical illustration

their investments prematurely, you will have to pay a surrender charge that makes up for their loss. During the surrender period, an annuity is not a demand deposit account like a savings or checking account. The higher returns that you are guaranteed from an annuity are dependent on the timeframe you selected. The longer an insurance company can hold your money, the easier it is for them to guarantee a predictable return on it.

If you leave your money in the annuity contract, you get a reliable monthly income no matter what happens in the market. Once the surrender period has expired, you can remove your money whenever you want. Your money becomes liquid again because the insurance company has used it in an investment that fit the timeline of your surrender period. For many people, this is an attractive trade off that can provide a creative solution for filling their income gap.

When is an annuity with an income rider right for you? A good financial professional can help you make that determination by taking the time to listen closely to your situation and understanding what your needs are as you enter retirement. Every salesperson has a bag full of brochures and PowerPoint presentations, but they need to know exactly what the financial concerns of their individual clients are in order to help them make the most informed and beneficial decision. Some people need income today, others need it in five or 10 years. Others may have their income needs met but are planning to move closer to their children and will need to buy a house in 10 years. Or, if you want income in 15 years, you might want to choose a different investment product for 10 years, and then switch to an annuity with an income rider during the last five years of your timeline. Everyone's situation is different and everyone's needs are different. People who are interested in annuities, however, usually need to make decisions that affect their income needs, whether it is filling their income gap, or providing for income down the road.

TWO INCOME ANNUITIES THAT WORK BEST

In Chapter Two we talked about Dark Green and Light Green Money. Annuities are the specific investment tools used to create these Green Money investments.

Annuity #1: Fixed Annuities are a Dark Green Money investments. These annuities are contracts with insurance companies and as such they have contractual guarantees within them. Fixed annuities are similar to the way a bank CD functions in that when you purchase the investment, the interest rate and duration is clearly stated, but fixed annuities usually offer more generous returns. You can choose a bank CD earning 1.7 percent for a 5 year period, or a fixed annuity earning 3 percent for that same 5 year period. The money in a fixed annuity also grows tax-deferred, which means you don't owe taxes on the gains until you pull the money out.

The downside of fixed annuities is that the interest rate is locked in. As such, you may miss out on an opportunity for higher growth during the time commitment when your annuity is locked into a fixed rate.

Annuity #2: Indexed Annuities are Light Green Money investments. Today's newest annuity is the Fixed Indexed Annuity, also known as the FIA and formerly known as the Equity Indexed annuity, or EIA. FIAs are a specialized type of annuity created in the middle to late '90s, known for their ability to generate earnings that are pretty substantial. As mentioned earlier, the key to how well these annuities perform is a feature known as Annual Reset. The worst you can do with a FIA is to make a zero gain. You can never go backwards. A Fixed Indexed Annuity *protects* the full amount that you contribute.

To help you understand the unique properties of an indexed investment, it helps to break the investment down according to these terms:

- *Equity:* refers to the amount of money you will put into the annuity. For example, if you have $150,000 saved in a 401(k), and you want to restructure that for a portion of your retirement income, your *equity* would be $150,000.
- *Indexed:* refers to how the annuity is keyed. It may be keyed to the S&P 500 or the Dow Jones Industrial Average or any number of indices. This is how the percentage on your rate of return is calculated. Although keyed to the market, FIAs are considered a Safe Money option because they have a guaranteed principal, meaning you can't lose money in this investment due to market loss.
- *Annuity:* the annual payout of an income.

When purchased with an income rider, FIAs can offer the income dependability of a paycheck controlled and administered by you. You choose the amount of money you put in, when to turn on the income stream, and for how long. They offer guaranteed principal, tax-deferred growth, lifetime income options and money to your beneficiaries.

SINGLE PREMIUM IMMEDIATE ANNUITIES (SPIA)

A single premium immediate annuity is simply a contract between you and an insurance company. SPIAs are structured so that you pay a lump sum of money (a single premium) to an insurance company, and they give you a guaranteed income over an agreed upon time period. That time period could be five years, or it could be for the remainder of your lifetime. Guarantees from insurance companies are based on the claims-paying ability of the issuing insurance company.

SPIAs provide investors with a stream of reliable income when they can't afford to take the risk of losing money in a fluctuating market. While there is general faith that the market always trends up, at least in the long-term, if you are focusing on income over a shorter period of time, you may not be able to take a big hit in the market. Beyond normal market volatility, interest rates also come with an inherent level of uncertainty, making it hard to create a dependable income on your own. SPIAs reduce risk for you by giving you regular monthly, quarterly or yearly payments that can begin the moment you buy the contract. Your financial professional can walk you through a series of different payment options to help you select the one that most closely fits your needs.

Additional Annuity Information:
- Some contracts will allow you to draw income from the high water mark that the market reaches each year. The income rider will then begin calculating its value from the high water mark.
- Income annuities are investment tools that look and feel a bit like Social Security. Every year you allow the money to grow with the market, and it will "roll up" by a specific amount, paying out a specific percent to you as income each year.
- Annuities can work very well to create income, and a financial professional can help you find the one that best matches your income need, and can also structure it to work perfectly for you.

THE RISK OF VARIABLE ANNUITIES

Variable annuities are a Red Money annuity that can lose money due to market fluctuations. As their name suggests, they vary with the stock market and the value of the principal is not guaranteed. If you discover that you have a variable annuity as part of your portfolio, you may want to have it reviewed because these annuities are known for having high fees. Because they are connected to multiple mutual funds, there is usually a fee attached to the management of each fund in addition to Mortality and Expense fees (listed as M&E fees) and administrative fees. The cost of these fees are often not easy to identify on your account statements, so many investors fail to consider the true cost of a variable annuity investment.

If your variable annuity has an income rider on it (and you may not even be aware of this,) the Income Account Value will stay the same or grow, but the value of your *actual* contract may fall. If you surrender the annuity, the insurance company will pay you the market value of the asset, regardless of whether it matches, exceeds or falls short of the value at which you bought the contract. If its value has dropped significantly, you may be better off taking the income rider as an income-for-life stream without surrendering your contract.

Just like any investment strategy, the amount of risk needs to fit the comfort level of the investor. Annuities are no exception. Without going into too much detail, here are some additional ways to manage risk with annuity options:

- Remember that variable annuities can lose money with market fluctuations. These annuities do not take advantage of annual reset when the market goes down. The income rider will stay the same, but the value of your actual contract may fall.
- If you want to structure an annuity investment for growth over a long period of time, be aware that the variable annuity option does not have principal guarantee protection. With a variable annuity, the value of your principal investment follows the market and can lose or gain value with the market. This type of annuity can also have an income rider, but it is really more useful as an accumulation tool that bets on an improving market. A 40-year-old couple, for example, will probably want to structure more for growth and take on more risk than someone in their 70s. The 40-year-old couple may select a variable annuity with

an income rider that kicks in when they plan to retire. If it rises with the market or outperforms it, the value of their investment has grown. If the market loses ground over the duration of the contract or their annuity underperforms, they can still rely on the income rider.

- If you are 68 years old and you have more immediate income needs that you need to come up with above and beyond your Social Security, you need a low risk, reliable source of income. If you choose an annuity option, you are looking for something that will pay out an income right away over a relatively short timeframe. You might want to opt for a SPIA that pays you immediately and spans a five year period, as well as an additional income annuity that begins paying you in five years, and another longer term annuity that begins paying you in 10 years.

- Bear in mind that each annuity contract has its own costs and fees. Review these with your financial professional before you determine the best products and strategies for your situation.

CREATING AN INCOME

Creating an income plan before you retire allows you to satisfy your need for lifetime income and ensures that your lifestyle can last as long as you do. You also want to create a plan that operates in the most efficient way possible. Doing so will give more security as you enter into the unknown void and will potentially allow you to build your legacy down the road. There are many strategies you can use to maximize the income streams from your annuity. One strategy using a multiple bucket approach involves multiple income creation products as shown in the following story:

> » *Keiko is 60 years old and is wondering how she can use her assets to provide her with a retirement income. She will*

be retiring in six years and has a $5,000 per month income need. If she starts withdrawing her Social Security benefit in six years at age 66, it will provide her with $2,200 per month. She also has a pension that kicks in at age 70 that will give her another $1,320 per month. That leaves her with two known income gaps: Gap #1 from ages 66 to 69 in the amount of $2,800. Gap #2 at the age of 70 and beyond in the amount of gap of $1,480. If Keiko uses only Light Green Money to solve her income need, she will need to deposit $918,360 at 2 percent interest to meet her monthly goal for her lifetime. If she opts to use Red Money and withdraws the amount she needs each month from the market, let's say the S & P 500, she will run out of cash in 10 years if she invested between the years of 2000 and 2012. Suffering a market downturn like that during the period for which she is relying on it for retirement income will change her life, and not for the better. Keiko wants her income to be safe and guaranteed.

Working with a financial professional and using a laddering strategy, Keiko is actually able to generate more income using less money. Her professional recommended two different income vehicles: one that allowed her to deposit just $190,161 in a Dark Green investment with a 2 percent return, and one that was a Light Green investment, or fixed indexed annuity. In the FIA she put $146,000, and because of the way the annuities were laddered, she was able to fill both income gaps using only $336,161, requiring her to spend $582,000 less money to accomplish her goal! Working with a professional to find the right tools for her retirement needs saved Keiko over half a million dollars.

Using annuities for income generation includes the following steps:

- Review your income needs and look specifically at the shortfall you may have during each year of your retirement based on your Social Security income, and income from any other assets you have.
- Ask yourself where you are in your payout or income phase. Is retirement one year away? 10 years away? Last year?
- Determine how much money you need and how you need to structure your existing assets to provide for that need.
- If you have an asset from which you need to generate income, consider options offered by purchasing an income rider on an annuity.

CHAPTER 5 RECAP //

- After Social Security and your additional income is accounted for, the amount that's left to meet your needs is called the *Income Gap*. Many retirees find that they have more than one income gap, including the gap that occurs in later years due to health issues, chronic illness or death of a spouse. An income annuity such as a fixed index annuity is one financial tool designed to solve these multiple income gaps.

- Although an indexed annuity is an income-producing asset that does not subject your income to market risk, it still has the opportunity to grow. Indexed annuities participate in market growth without market loss through an indexing strategy. This combined with the power of annual reset gives you both growth and the guaranteed safety of your principal.

- The benefits of an indexed income annuity include: guarantee of principal, a minimum guaranteed cash value, no fees, access to your money, bonus money, tax deferral, and a guaranteed lifetime income.

- Be sure you understand the features, benefits, costs and fees associated with any annuity product before you invest.

6

GETTING OUT OF
THE BLACK HOLE

*"Mr. Spock, the women on your planet are logical. That's the only
planet in the galaxy that can make that claim."*
— Captain Kirk, Star Trek: The Original Series

While the above quote is specific to an imaginary world, it could
be said that in our world, both women and men find themselves
making many illogical decisions when it comes to the stock market and their portfolios. When you are managing your money by
yourself, emotions inevitably enter into the mix. The Dow Jones
Industrial Average and the S&P 500 represent more to you than
market fluctuations. They represent your retirement goals. It's
hard not to be emotional about it.

Everyone knows you should buy low and sell high. But this is what is more likely to happen:

The market takes a downturn, similar to the 2008 crash, and investors see as much as a 30 percent loss in their stock holdings. It's hard to watch, and it's harder to bear the pain of losing that much money. The sequence of returns means that if they retire in the years directly before or after the loss, their funds have a much greater chance of dwindling quickly, with no chance of recuperation. So they sell and hope to preserve what's left. But eventually, and inevitably, the market begins to rise again. Maybe slowly, maybe with some moderate growth, but by the time the average investor notices an upward trend and wants to buy in again, they have already missed a great deal of the gains.

> *» Beverly worked for a film studio for 34 years. During her time there, she acquired bonuses and pay raises that often included shares of stock in the production company. She also dedicated part of her paycheck every month to a 401(k) that bought stock in the company. By the time she retired, Beverly has $250,000 worth of company stock.*
>
> *Although she had contributed to her 401(k) account every month, Beverly didn't cultivate any other assets that could generate income for her during retirement. Beverly also retired early at age 62 because of her failing health. The commute to Los Angeles every day was becoming difficult in her weakened condition and she wanted to enjoy the rest of her life in retirement instead of working the long hours at the film studio.*
>
> *Because she retired early, Beverly failed to maximize her Social Security benefit. While she lives a modest lifestyle, her income needs are $3,500 per month. Beverly's monthly Social Security check only covers $1,900, leaving her with a $1,600 income gap. To supplement her Social Security check, Beverly sells $1,600 of company stock each month*

to meet her income needs. A $250,000 401(k) is nothing to sneeze at, but reducing its value by $1,600 every month will decimate her savings within 10 years. And that's if the market stays neutral or grows modestly. If the market takes a downturn, the money that Beverly relies on to fill her income gap will rapidly diminish. Even if the market starts going up in a couple of years, it will take much larger gains for her to recover the value that she lost due to the math of rebounds (which will be explained shortly).

Unhappily for Beverly, she retired in 2007, just before the major market downturn that lasted for several years. She lost more than 20 percent of the value of her stock. Because Beverly needed to sell her stock to meet her basic income needs, the market price of the stock was secondary to her need for the money. When she needed money, she was forced to sell however many shares she needed to fill her income gap that month. And if she has a financial crisis, involving a need for long term medical care, for example, she will be forced to sell stock even if the market is low and her shares are nearly worthless.

Beverly realizes that she could have relied on an investment structured to deliver her a regular income while protecting the value of her investment. She could have kept her $250,000 from diminishing while enjoying her lifestyle into retirement regardless of the volatility of the market. Ideally, Beverly would have restructured her 401(k) to reflect the level of risk that she was able to take. In her case, she would have had most of her money in a Safe Money assets, allowing her to rely on the value of her assets when she needed them.

THE ARGUMENT FOR A VULCANIZED PORTFOLIO

In the Star Trek series, it was the character of Spock who was known best for his calculated and logical decisions. As a Vulcan, he had the kind of brain that could compute numbers and then adjust his behavior accordingly, even if it went against what his emotions told him to do. We humans aren't as adept at following Vulcan ways.

In 2013, DALBAR, the well-respected financial services market research firm, released their annual "Quantitative Analysis of Investment Behavior" report (QAIB). The report studied the impact of market volatility on individual investors: people like Beverly, or anyone who was managing (or mismanaging) their own investments in the stock market.

According to the study, volatility not only caused investors to make decisions based on their emotions, those decisions also harmed their investments and prevented them from realizing potential gains. So why do people meddle so much with their investments when the market is fluctuating? Part of the reason is that many people have financial obligations that they don't have control over. Significant expenses like house payments, the unexpected cost of replacing a broken-down car, and medical bills can put people in a position where they need money. If they need to sell investments to come up with that money, they don't have the luxury of selling when they *want* to. They must sell when they *need* to.

DALBAR's "Quantitative Analysis of Investor Behavior" has been used to measure the effects of investors' buying, selling and mutual fund switching decisions since 1994. The QAIB shows time and time again over nearly a 20 year period that the average investor earns less, and in many cases, significantly less than the performance of mutual funds suggests. QAIB's goal is to improve independent investor performance and to help financial professionals provide helpful advice and investment strategies that address the concerns and behaviors of the average investor.

An excerpt from the report claims that:

"QAIB offers guidance on how and where investor behaviors can be improved. No matter what the state of the mutual fund industry, boom or bust: Investment results are more dependent on investor behavior than on fund performance. Mutual fund investors who hold on to their investments are more successful than those who time the market.

QAIB uses data from the Investment Company Institute (ICI), Standard & Poor's and Barclays Capital Index Products to compare mutual fund investor returns to an appropriate set of benchmarks.

There are actually three primary causes for the chronic shortfall for both equity and fixed income investors:

1. *Capital not available to invest. This accounts for 25 percent to 35 percent of the shortfall.*
2. *Capital needed for other purposes. This accounts for 35 percent to 45 percent of the shortfall.*
3. *Psychological factors. These account for 45 percent to 55 percent of the shortfall."*

The key findings of Dalbar's QAIB report provide compelling statistics about how individual investment strategies produced negative outcomes for the majority of investors:

- Psychological factors account for 45 percent to 55 percent of the chronic investment return shortfall for both equity and fixed income investors.
- Asset allocation is designed to handle the investment decision-making for the investor, which can materially reduce the shortfall due to psychological factors.
- Successful asset allocation investing requires investors to act on two critical imperatives:
  a. Balance capital preservation and appreciation so that they are aligned with the investor's objective.
  b. Select a qualified allocator.

- The best way for an investor to determine their risk tolerance is to utilize a risk tolerance assessment. However, these assessments must be accessible and usable.
- Evaluating allocator quality requires analysis of the allocator's underlying investments, decision making process and whether or not past efforts have produced successful outcomes.
- Choosing a top allocator makes a significant difference in the investment results one will achieve.
- Mutual fund retention rates suggest that the average investor has not remained invested for long enough periods to derive the potential benefits of the investment markets.
- Retention rates for asset allocation funds exceed those of equity and fixed income funds by over a year.
- Investors' ability to correctly time the market is highly dependent on the direction of the market. Investors generally guess right more often in up markets. However, in 2012 investors guessed right only 42 percent of the time during a bull market.
- Analysis of investor fund flows compared to market performance further supports the argument that investors are unsuccessful at timing the market. Market upswings rarely coincide with mutual fund inflows while market downturns do not coincide with mutual fund outflows.
- Average equity mutual fund investors gained 15.56 percent compared to a gain of 15.98 percent that just holding the S&P 500 produced.
- The shortfall in the long-term annualized return of the average mutual fund equity investor and the S&P 500 continued to decrease in 2012.
- The fixed-income investor experienced a return of 4.68 percent compared to an advance of 4.21 percent on the Barclays Aggregate Bond Index.

- The average fixed income investor has failed to keep up with inflation in nine out of the last 14 years.*

It doesn't take a financial services market research report to tell you that market volatility is out of your control. The report does prove, however, that before you experience market volatility, you should have an investment plan, and when the market is fluctuating, you should stand by your investment plan. You should also review and discuss your investment plan with your financial professional on a regular basis, ensuring he/she is aware of any changes in your goals, financial circumstances, your health or your risk tolerance. When the economy is under stress and the markets are volatile, investors can feel vulnerable. That vulnerability causes people to tinker with their portfolios in an attempt to outsmart the market. Financial professionals, however, don't try to time the market for their clients. They try to tap into the gains that can be realized by committing to long-term investment strategies.

WILL YOUR ENTERPRISE RUN OUT OF FUEL?

We mentioned the sequence of returns earlier in Chapter Two, but it bears mentioning again here. Regular withdrawals from your account combined with unfortunate market timing can do more than just deplete your savings—it can increase the chances that you will run out of money. The sequence of returns shows us that even more than the actual rate of return, it is the order of the market loss as it relates to your retirement timeline that can cause the most damage to your portfolio.

Consider the following chart. Both John and Susan started with the same balance of $500,000 when they retired; both retirees withdrew money at a rate of 5 percent and both received the exact same 8.3 rate of return during a 20 year period. However,

---

* 2013 QAIB, Dalbar, March 2013

	John				Susan		
Age	Hypothetical stock market gains or losses	Withdrawal at start of year	Nest Egg at start of year	Age	Hypothetical stock market gains or losses	Withdrawal at start of year	Nest Egg at start of year
64			$500,000	64			$500,000
65	-10.14%	$25,000	$500,000	65	12.78%	$25,000	$500,000
66	-13.04%	$25,750	$426,839	66	23.45%	$25,750	$535,716
67	-23.37%	$26,523	$348,776	67	26.38%	$26,523	$629,575
68	14.62%	$27,318	$246,956	68	3.53%	$27,318	$762,140
69	2.03%	$28,138	$251,750	69	13.62%	$28,138	$760,755
70	12.40%	$28,982	$228,146	70	3.00%	$28,982	$832,396
71	27.25%	$29,851	$223,862	71	-38.49%	$29,851	$827,524
72	-6.56%	$30,747	$246,879	72	26.38%	$30,747	$490,684
73	26.31%	$31,669	$201,956	73	19.53%	$31,669	$581,270
74	4.46%	$32,619	$215,084	74	26.67%	$32,619	$656,916
75	7.06%	$33,598	$190,610	75	31.01%	$33,598	$790,788
76	-1.54%	$34,606	$168,090	76	20.26%	$34,606	$991,981
77	34.11%	$35,644	$131,429	77	34.11%	$35,644	$1,151,375
78	20.26%	$36,713	$128,458	78	-1.54%	$36,713	$1,496,314
79	31.01%	$37,815	$110,335	79	7.06%	$37,815	$1,437,133
80	26.67%	$38,949	$95,008	80	4.46%	$38,949	$1,498,042
81	19.53%	$40,118	$71,009	81	26.31%	$40,118	$1,524,231
82	26.38%	$36,923	$36,923	82	-6.56%	$41,321	$1,874,535
83	-38.49%	$0	$0	83	27.25%	$42,561	$1,712,970
84	3.00%			84	12.40%	$43,838	$2,125,604
85	13.62%			85	2.03%	$45,153	$2,339,923
86	3.53%			86	14.62%	$46,507	$2,341,297
87	26.38%			87	-23.37%	$47,903	$2,630,297
88	23.45%			88	-13.04%	$49,340	$1,978,993
89	12.78%			89	-10.14%	$50,820	$1,677,975

The above chart is a hypothetical example created by the author to illustrate the concept of sequence of return.

John ran out of money at the age of 83, whereas Susan's account at that age was still going strong. By the time she went on to meet her maker at the age of 89, her account balance was worth over one and a half million dollars.

This huge discrepancy is due to the sequence of returns. The only thing we did differently was to reverse the order of the returns received by each investor. John took three big hits at the beginning of his retirement, whereas Susan took those hits at the end of her retirement. How will your gains be calculated? Well that all depends on how the market performs, and the order in which it performs. You may have the same $500,000 as a starting principal, with an annual withdrawal rate of 5 percent and an average rate of return at 8.3 percent, but it is the sequence of returns that dictates what your final balance will be.

There's no way around it; people get emotional about their money. And for good reason. You've spent your life working for it, exchanging your time and talent for it, and making decisions about how to invest it, save it and make it grow. The maintenance of your lifestyle and your plans for retirement all depend on it. The best investment strategies, however, don't rely on emotions.

When considering stock market investments and equities during your retirement years, be sure to factor in the math of rebounds and the sequence of returns when making your decision. Unless you are always as logical as a Vulcan, remember that the average investor going it alone is likely to earn less than a 2.6 percent rate of return. You have no control over world events, the behavior of politicians, CEOs or celebrities. You DO have control over the allocation of your assets.

CHAPTER 6 RECAP //

- The timing of market downturns is more critical to retirees than to the average investor. If you are making withdrawals on a market investment without principal guarantees, and the account suffers a loss, the math of rebounds dictates that rapid depletion of your funds will change what the future of your retirement looks like.

- The sequence of returns tells us that in addition to how the market performs, the order of those returns is just as important when it comes to calculating the value of your account.

- Emotions inevitably enter the mix during stock market downturns. According to the DALBAR "Quantitative Analysis of Investment Behavior" report released in 2013, the average fixed income investor managing their money alone failed to keep up with inflation in nine out of the last 14 years.

- Financial professionals don't try to outsmart the market when managing investments for their clients. Instead, they tap into the potential for gains by committing to proven and long-term investment strategies.

7

ENTERPRISE SHIELDS:
INDEXING FOR INFLATION

"The truth is usually just an excuse for a lack of imagination."
— Elim Garak, *Star Trek: Deep Space Nine*

Throughout the book, we have discussed how today, investment options require advice that is relevant to today. Traditional, outdated investment strategies are not only ineffective; they can be harmful to the average investor. One of the most traditional ways of thinking about investing is the risk versus reward trade-off. It goes something like this:

Investment options that are considered safer carry less risk, but also offer the potential for less return. Riskier investment options carry the burden of volatility and a greater potential for loss, but they also offer a greater potential for large rewards. Most professionals move their clients back and forth along this range, shifting between investments that are safer and investments that are structured for growth. Essentially, the old rules of investing dictate that you can either choose relative safety *or* return, but you can't have both.

Updated investment strategies work with the flexibility of liquidity to remake the rules. Here is how:

There are three dimensions that are inherent in any investment: *Liquidity, Safety,* and *Return.* You can maximize any two of these dimensions at the expense of the third. If you choose Safety and Liquidity, this is like keeping your assets in a checking account or savings account. This option delivers a lot of Safety and Liquidity, but at the expense of any Return. On the other hand, if you choose Liquidity and Return, meaning you have the potential for great return and can still reclaim your money whenever you choose, you will likely be exposed to a very high level of risk.

One strategy we employ is to put more than one income annuity product together in what is known as a *laddering* strategy. Laddering multiple income creation tools set for specific time periods can structure income for 10, 15 or 20 years and more down the road, allowing you to index for inflation. If inflation is low or you don't need the extra income, you don't have to turn the income spigot on. When expenses do go up, you turn on the income stream and relax, knowing your finances are secured. These investments act as shields to protect your retirement enterprise from the risk of rising prices, health care expenses and long term care costs.

The more protected your vehicle, the safer your journey will be.

» *Tiberius had over $1 million in assets, but his portfolio was set up in a very inefficient tax manner. He wanted to retire but had just taken a hit in the stock market. Tiberius didn't want to watch any more of his money disappear into the black hole of the stock market so he made an appointment* *with a financial professional who specialized in retirement planning.*

The financial professional showed how to restructure his portfolio by separating his investments into six different buckets. Utilizing separate buckets of money allowed him to structure tax efficient income while securing safety and growth. The issue of liquidity was solved by establishing an emergency fund and setting long term buckets that would be annuitized in ten years' time.

In the first bucket, Tiberius invested in a Single Premium Immediate Annuity (SPIA) that would provide him with $14,000 of safe, guaranteed income a year for the next 10 years. That amount combined with his Social Security benefit (also indexed for inflation) allowed him to eliminate his Social Security tax while continuing to grow the rest of his money tax deferred. In fact, over the next ten years, Tiberius was able to receive $1,400 a month in tax free income.

When the first bucket of money runs out, he will turn on bucket number two: a Light Green income annuity that will give him a pay raise by providing $1,820 of income each month. This annuity also has an income rider providing a joint payout for both Tiberius and his spouse so the income is guaranteed to never run out. They are also able to access 10 percent of the account balance should a need for additional liquidity arise. In a third bucket he has another way to safely increase his income by another $410 a month when he turns 80. Meanwhile, Tiberius has other buckets growing that will mature in 10 years' time, giving him the freedom to access large lump sums of money should the need arise.

Now, Tiberius and his wife only pay taxes on half of their income, while the other half is tax free, and they are shielded from inflation. By separating their investments into separate buckets, they are able to capitalize on all three components of growth, safety and liquidity.

If you have the option of putting your money in a long-term investment, you will be sacrificing Liquidity, but potentially gaining both Safety and Return. By laddering your investments, you can increase your opportunities for liquidity without sacrificing safety or growth. Rethinking your approach to money in this way can make a world of difference and can provide you with a structured way to generate income while allowing the value of your asset to grow over time.

The question is, how much Liquidity do you *really* need? Think about it. If you haven't sat down and created an income plan for your retirement, your perceived need for Liquidity is a guess. You don't know how much cash you'll need to fill the income gap if you don't know the amount of your Social Security benefit of the total of your other income options. If you *have* determined your income need and have made a plan for filling your income gap, you can partition your assets based on when you will need them. With an income plan in place, *you can use new rules to enjoy both Safety and Return from your assets.*

CHAPTER 7 RECAP //

- The three aspects of any investment include liquidity, safety, and return. You can choose to maximize any two against the third.
- Choosing to maximize liquidity alone can be an expensive option because the sooner you need your money back, the less you can leverage it for safety and return.
- To plan for a successful retirement in today's economy requires a creative use of today's financial tools.

8

DEEP SPACE PROTECTION:
TAXES AND RETIREMENT

"Perhaps we need a good kick in our complacency to get us ready for what's ahead."

— Captain Picard, Star Trek: The Next Generation

Everyone is familiar with taxes (you've been paying them your entire working life), but not everyone is familiar with how to make tax planning a part of their retirement strategy.

Tax planning and *tax reporting* are two very different things. Most people only *report* their taxes. March rolls around, people pull out their 1040s or use TurboTax to enter their income and taxable assets, and ship it off to Uncle Sam at the IRS. If you use a CPA to report your taxes, you are essentially paying them to record history. You have the option of being proactive with your taxes and to plan for your future by making smart, informed decisions about how taxes affect your overall financial plan. Working with a financial professional who, along with a CPA, makes recommendations about your finances to you, will keep you looking forward and protect you from the dangers of deep space as you travel through retirement.

PAYING LESS TAX DURING YOUR RETIREMENT

When you retire, you move from the earning and accumulation phase of your life into the asset distribution phase of your life. For most people, that means relying on Social Security, a 401(k), an IRA, or a pension. Wherever you have put your Green Money for retirement, you are going to start relying on it to provide you with the income that once came as a paycheck. Most of these distributions will be considered income by the IRS and will be taxed as such. There are exceptions to that (not all of your Social Security income is taxed, and income from Roth IRAs is not taxed), but for the most part, your distributions will be subject to income taxes.

Regarding assets that you have in an IRA or a 401(k) plan that uses an IRA, when you reach 70 ½ years of age, you will be required to draw a certain amount of money from your IRA as income each year. That amount depends on your age and the balance in your IRA. The amount that you are required to withdraw as income is called a Required Minimum Distribution (RMD). Why are you required to withdraw money from your own account? Chances are the money in that account has grown over time, and the government wants to collect taxes on that growth. If you have a large balance in an IRA, there's a chance your RMD could increase your income significantly enough to put you into a higher tax bracket, subjecting you to a higher tax rate.

Here's where tax planning can really begin to work strongly in your favor. In the distribution phase of your life, you have a predictable income based on your RMDs, your Social Security benefit and any other income-generating assets you may have. What really impacts you at this stage is how much of that money you keep in your pocket after taxes. Essentially, *you will make more money saving on taxes than you will by making more money.* If you can reduce your tax burden by 30, 20 or even 10 percent, you earn yourself that much more money by not paying it in taxes.

How do you save money on taxes? By having a plan. In this instance, a financial professional can work with the CPAs at their firm to create a **distribution plan** that minimizes your taxes and maximizes your annual net income.

BUILDING A TAX DIVERSIFIED PORTFOLIO

So far so good: avoid taxes, maximize your net annual income and have a plan for doing it. When people decide to leverage the experience and resources of a financial professional, they may not be thinking of how distribution planning and tax planning will benefit their portfolios. Often more exciting prospects like planning income annuities, investing in the market and structuring investments for growth rule the day. Taxes, however, play a crucial role in retirement planning. Achieving those tax goals requires knowledge of options, foresight and professional guidance.

Finding the path to a good tax plan isn't always a simple task. Every tax return you file is different from the one before it because things constantly change. Your expenses change. Planned or unplanned purchases occur. Health care costs, medical bills, an inheritance, property purchases, reaching an age where your RMD kicks in or travel, any number of things can affect how much income you report and how many deductions you take each year.

Preparing for the ever-changing landscape of your financial life requires a tax-diversified portfolio that can be leveraged to balance the incomes, expenditures and deductions that affect you each year. A financial professional will work with you to answer questions like these:

- What does your tax landscape look like?
- Do you have a tax-diversified portfolio robust enough to adapt to your needs?
- Do you have a diversity of taxable and non-taxable income planned for your retirement?
- Will you be able to maximize your distributions to take advantage of your deductions when you retire?
- Is your portfolio strong enough and tax-diversified enough to adapt to an ever-changing (and usually increasing) tax code?

» *When Lily returns home after a week in the hospital recovering from a knee replacement, the 77-year-old calls her daughter, sister and brother to let them know she is home and feeling well. She also should have called her CPA. Lily's medical expenses for the procedure, her hospital stay, her medications and the ongoing physical therapy she attended amount to more than $50,000.*

Currently, Americans can deduct medical expenses that are more than 7.5 percent of their Adjusted Gross Income (AGI). Lily's AGI is $60,000 the year of her knee replacement, meaning she is able to deduct $44,000 of her medical bills from her taxes that year. Her AGI dictated that she could deduct more than 80 percent of her medical expenses that year. **Lily didn't know this.**

Had she been working with a financial professional who regularly asked her about any changes in her life, her spending, or her expenses (expected or unexpected), Lily could have saved thousands of dollars. Lily can also file an amendment to her tax return to recoup the overpayment.

This relatively simple example of how tax planning can save you money is just the tip of the iceberg. No one can be expected to know the entire U.S. tax code. But a professional who is working with a team of CPAs and financial professionals have an advantage over the average taxpayer who must start from square one on their own every year. Have you been taking advantage of all the deductions that are available to you?

PROACTIVE TAX PLANNING

The implications of proactive tax planning are far reaching, and are larger than many people realize. Remember, doing your taxes in January, February, March or April means you are writing a history book. Planning your taxes in October, November or December means that you are writing the story as it happens. You can look at all the factors that are at play and make decisions that will impact your tax return *before* you file it.

Realizing that tax planning is an aspect of financial planning is an important leap to make. When you incorporate tax planning into your financial planning strategy, it becomes part of the way you maximize your financial potential. Paying less in taxes means you keep more of your money. Simply put, the more money you keep, the more of it you can leverage as an asset. This kind of planning can affect you at any stage of your life. If you are 40 years old, are you contributing the maximum amount to your 401(k) plan? Are you contributing to a Roth IRA? Are you finding ways to structure the savings you are dedicating to your children's education? Do you have life insurance? Taxes and tax planning affects all of these investment tools. Having a relationship with a professional who works with a CPA can help you build a truly comprehensive financial plan that not only works with your investments, but also shapes your assets to find the most efficient ways to prepare for tax time. There may be years that you could benefit from higher distributions because of the tax bracket that you are in, or there could be years you would benefit from taking less. There may be years when you have a lot of deductions and years you have relatively few. **Adapting your distributions to work in concert with your available deductions** is at the heart of smart tax planning. Professional guidance can bring you to the next level of income distribution, allowing you to remain flexible enough to maximize your tax efficiency. And remember, saving money on taxes makes you more money than making money does.

What you have on paper is important: your assets, savings, investments, which are financial expression of your work and time. It's just as important to know how to get it off the paper in a way that keeps most of it in your pocket. Almost anything that involves financial planning also involves taxes. Annuities, investments, IRAs, 401(k)s, 403(b), and many other investment options will have tax implications. Life also has a way of throwing curveballs. Illness, expensive car repair or replacement, or *any event that has a financial impact on your life will likely have a corresponding tax implication* around which you should adapt your financial plan. Tax planning does just that.

One dollar can end up being less than 25 cents to your heirs.

» *When Data's father passed away, he discovered that he was the beneficiary of his father's $500,000 IRA. Data has a wife and a family of four children, and he knew that his father had intended for a large portion of the IRA to go toward funding their college educations.*

After Data's father's estate is distributed, Data, who is 50 years old and whose two oldest sons are entering college, liquidates the IRA. By doing so, his taxable income for that year puts him in a 39.6 percent tax bracket, immediately reducing the value of the asset to $302,000. An additional 3.8 percent surtax on net investment income further diminishes the funds *to $283,000. Liquidating the IRA in effect subjects much of Data's regular income to the surtax, as well. At this point, Data will be taxed at 43.4 percent.*

Data's state taxes are an additional 9 percent. Moreover, estate taxes on Data's father's assets claim another 22 percent. By the time the IRS is through, Data's income from the IRA will be taxed at 75 percent, leaving him with $125,000 of the original $500,000. While it would help contribute to the education of his children, it wouldn't come anywhere near completely paying for it, something the $500,000 could have easily done.

As the above example makes clear, leaving an asset to your beneficiaries can be more complicated than it may seem. In the case of a traditional IRA, after federal, estate and state taxes, the asset could literally diminish to as little as 25 percent of its value.

How does working with a professional help you make smarter tax decisions with your own finances? Any financial professional worth their salt will be working with a firm that has a team of trained tax professionals, including CPAs, who have an intimate knowledge of the tax code and how to adapt a financial plan to it.

Here's another example of how taxes have major implications on asset management:

> *» Wesley and Christine, a 62-year-old couple, begin working with a financial professional in October. After structuring their assets to reflect their risk tolerance and creating assets that would provide them income during retirement, they feel good about their situation. They make decisions that allow them to maximize their Social Security benefits, they have plenty of options for filling their income gaps, and they have a strategy in place that counters inflation and gives them growth opportunities. When their professional asks them*

about their tax plan, they tell him their CPA handled their taxes every year, and did a great job. Their professional says, "I don't mean who does your taxes, I mean, who does your tax planning?" Wesley and Christine aren't sure how to respond.

Their professional brings Wesley and Christine's financial plan to the firm's CPA and has her run a tax projection for them. A week later their professional calls them with a tax plan for the year that will save them more than $3,000 on their tax return. The couple is shocked. A simple piece of advice from the CPA based on the numbers revealed that if they paid their estimated taxes before the end of the year, they would be able to itemize it as a deduction, allowing them to save thousands of dollars.

This solution won't work for everyone, and it may not work for Wesley and Christine every year. That's not the point. By being proactive with their approach to taxes and using the resources made available by their financial professional, they were able to create a tax plan that saved them money.

ESTATE TAXES

The government doesn't just tax your income from investments while you're alive. They will also dip into your legacy.

While estate taxes aren't as hot of a topic as they were a few years ago, they are still an issue of concern for many people with assets. While taxes may not apply on estates that are less than $5 million, certain states have estate taxes with much lower exclusion ratios. Some are as low as $600,000. Many people may have to pay a state estate tax. One strategy for avoiding those types of taxes is to move assets outside of your estate. That can include gifting them to family or friends, or putting them into an irrevocable trust. Life insurance is another option for protecting your legacy.

CHAPTER 8 RECAP //

- When you report your taxes, you are paying to record history. When you *plan* your taxes with a financial professional, you are proactively finding the best options for your tax return. Knowing how to use tax law in your favor means putting more money in your wallet and less money into the hands of Uncle Sam.

- It's important to understand the tax repercussions when tapping into assets from a 401(k) or a traditional IRA for use an income source. Money that is considered qualified by the Federal government must be taxed upon distribution.

- At the age of 70 ½, the Federal Government requires all IRA participants to take their RMD, or Required Minimum Distribution. Failure to take your RMD can cost you thousands of dollars in taxes and penalty fees.

- Taxes play an important role during your retirement. It's important that you understand your obligations, and the differences between tax-deferred and tax-advantaged advantaged accounts.

- You make more money by saving on taxes than you do by making more money. This simple concept becomes extremely valuable to people in retirement and those living on fixed incomes.

9

PREPARING FOR WHAT'S AHEAD: THE FUTURE OF U.S. TAXATION

"Logic is the beginning of wisdom; not the end."
– Captain Spock, *Star Trek VI: The Undiscovered Country*

Tax legislation over the course of American history has left one very resounding message: taxes go up. Sadly, we hear this same threat so often that it has begun to sound like the boy who cried wolf. The reason behind this lies in the fact that tax hikes usually do not take effect until two or three years after their introduction and subsequently get piecemeal implementation. The result of this prolonged implementation period can be equated to death by a thousand paper cuts.

DEBT CEILING – CAUSE AND EFFECTS

The raising of the debt ceiling raised more than just the ability for our government to go further into debt. It also raised concerns and fears about the future of our economy. We are now seeing major swings in the markets with investors showing serious concerns over the future of investment valuations and their personal wealth. Unfortunately, the reasoning behind all of this uncertainty is preceded by the inability to see the full implications of what is in store. We rarely talk about the fact that the discussions on raising the debt ceiling were coupled to discussions on major tax reforms needed to correct the problems underlining the debt ceiling increase itself.

Increasing the debt ceiling was needed because the government maxed out its credit card, so to speak, which it has been living off of for quite some time. It is really not much different than what we have been seeing from the general public for the past few decades. Unfortunately, most of us do not have the ability to get a credit limit increase on our credit cards once we reach the maximum limit, that is unless we can show the ability to pay this balance back. The only way to pay this credit card back is by spending less and making more money.

This is exactly where the federal government is today. They have been given a higher credit limit, but they still must find a way to decrease the spending while making more money. The only way the government makes money is by collecting taxes.

Unfortunately, at the current moment, the government is collecting approximately $120 billion less per month than it currently spends. Discussions for major tax reform have accompanied the discussions for the increased debt ceiling.

DEBT AND EARNINGS

Let us take a closer look at where we are today. The U.S. national debt is increasing at an alarming rate, rising to levels never seen before and threatening serious harm to the economy. Through the end of 2010, the national debt had risen to $13.6 trillion, averaging an 11.4 percent increase annually over the past five years and a 9.2 percent increase annually over the past 10 years. To put this into perspective, the national gross domestic product (GDP) has increased to $14.5 trillion during the same period, averaging a 2.9 percent annual increase over the past five years and a 3.9 percent increase over the past 10 years. At the end of 2010, the national debt level was 93 percent of the GDP. Economists believe that a sustainable economy exists at a maximum level of approximately 80 percent. As of December 20, 2013, the U.S. national debt was 107.69 percent of GDP with the debt at $17.252 trillion and the GDP at $16.020 trillion.*

The significance of these two numbers lies within the contrast. The national debt is the amount that needs to be repaid. This is the credit card balance. Gross domestic product on the other hand is less known and represents the market value of all final goods and services produced within a country during a given period. Essentially, GDP represents the gross taxable income available to the government. If debts are increasing at a greater rate than the gross income available for taxation, then the only way to make up the difference is by increasing the rate at which the gross income is taxed.

The most recent presidential budget shows a continuing trend in the disparity between growth in the national debt and GDP over the next two decades. Although the increasing disparity is a real concern and shows that, at least in the short run, the federal deficit will not be addressed to counteract the potential crisis ahead, it is the revenue collection that tells the disconcerting story. Over the past 40 years the average collection of GDP has

---

* *http://www.usdebtclock.org/ 12/20/13*

been approximately 17.6 percent and currently collections are at approximately 14.4 percent of GDP.

As the presidential budget reveals, the projected revenues are estimated to be 20 percent by the end of the next decade. That is a 38.8 percent increase from the current tax levels. To put this into perspective, if you are currently in the top tax bracket of 35 percent and this bracket increases by the proposed collection increase, your tax rate will be approximately 48.5 percent. Keep in mind that even at this rate the deficit is projected to increase.

2013 – THE END OF AN ERA?

As the graph below shows, from a historical point of view, the federal income tax is extremely low. The last time the U.S. national debt was at the same percentage level of GDP as today was at the end of World War II and several years following. The maximum tax rate averaged 90 percent from 1944 through 1963. Compare that to the maximum rate of 35 percent today and it becomes very clear that there is a disparity of extreme proportion.

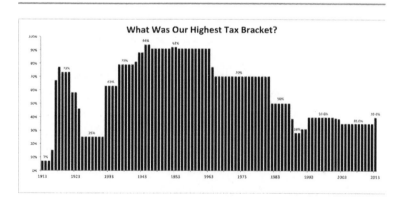

The author created this graph using federal income tax data found at the following source: http:// taxfoundation.org/article/us-federal-individual-income-tax-rates-history-1913-2013-nominal- and-inflation-adjusted-brackets

Taxes during this historical period were at extreme levels for nearly 20 years, during and following this current level of debt-to-GDP. A significant point to note about the difference between that time and today is the economic activity. The period of 1944 through 1963 was in the heart of both the industrial revolution and the birth of the Baby Boom generation. Today, we are mired in extreme volatility with frequent periods of boom and bust at the same time we are witnessing the beginning of the greatest retirement wave ever experienced within the U.S. economy.

To contrast these two time periods in respect to the recovery period is almost asinine as the external pressures from globalization and domestic unfunded liabilities did not exist or were irrelevant factors during the prior period.

To add insult to injury, U.S. domestic unfunded liabilities are currently estimated somewhere around $61.6 trillion due to items such as Social Security, Medicare and government pensions. The most concerning part of this pertains to the coming wave of retirement as the Baby Boom generation begins retiring and drawing on the unfunded Social Security for which they currently have entitlement. Over the long run, expenditures related to healthcare programs such as Medicare and Medicaid are projected to grow faster than the economy overall as the population matures.

To put unfunded liabilities into perspective, consider these as off-balance-sheet obligations similar to those of Enron. Although these are not listed as part of the national debt, they must be paid. These liabilities exist outside of the annual budgetary debt discussed. The difference between Enron and the U.S. unfunded liabilities is that if the U.S. government cannot come up with the funds to pay all these liabilities through revenue generation, they will print the money necessary to pay the debt.

WHAT DOES THE SOLUTION LOOK LIKE?

Unfortunately, the general public is in a no-win situation for this solution to the problem. Printing money does not bode well for economic growth. This creates inflationary pressures that devalue the U.S. dollar and make everyone less wealthy. Cutting the entitlements that compose this liability leaves millions of people without benefits they have come to expect. The only other option, and one that the government knows all too well, is increasing taxes. In fact, according to a Congressional Budget Office paper issued in 2004:

"The term 'unfunded liability' has been used to refer to a gap between the government's projected financial commitment under a particular program and the revenues that are expected to be available to fund that commitment. But no government obligation can be truly considered 'unfunded' because of the U.S. government's sovereign power to tax—which is the ultimate resource to meet its obligations."

A balanced budget will be required at some point and with this will come higher taxes. We have uncertainty surrounding tax rates and how high they will go. At that time, extensions put in place in December 2010 on Bush-era tax cuts are set to expire. We are likely to see some tax increases at this point. Whether it is only on the top earners or unilaterally across all income levels is yet to be seen, but an increase of some sort will most certainly occur.

How do you prepare? Why spend so much time reassuring you that taxes will increase? Because you have an opportunity to take action. Now is the time to prepare for what will come and structure countermeasures for the good, the bad and the ugly of each of these legislative nightmares through tax-advantaged retirement planning.

You make more money by saving on taxes than you do by making more money. The simplistic logic of the statement makes sense when you discover it takes $1.50 in earnings to put that same dollar, saved in taxes, back in your pocket.

As simple as it sounds, it is much more difficult to execute. Most people fail to put together a plan as they near retirement, beginning with a simple cash flow budget. If you have not analyzed your proposed income streams and expenses, you could not possibly have taken the time to position these cash flows and other events into a tax-preferred plan.

Most people will state that they have a plan and, thus, do not need any further assistance in this area. The truth in most instances is that people could not show you their plan, and among the few that could, most would not be able to show you how they have executed it. In this regard, they might as well be Richard Nixon stating, "I am not a crook" for as much as they state, "I have a plan." The truth lies in waiting. As we approach or begin retirement, we should look at what cash flows we will have. Do we have a pension? How about Social Security? How much additional cash flow am I going to need to draw from my assets to maintain the lifestyle that I desire?

We spend our whole lives saving and accumulating wealth but spend so little time determining how to distribute this accumulation so as to retain it. We need to make sure we have the appropriate diversification of taxable versus non-taxable assets to complement our distribution strategy.

THE BENEFITS OF DIVERSIFICATION

Heading into retirement, we should be situated with a diversified tax landscape. The point to spending our whole lives accumulating wealth is not to see the size of the number on paper, but rather to be an exercise in how much we put in our pocket after removing it from the paper. To truly understand tax diversification, we must understand what types of money exist and how each of these will be treated during accumulation and, most importantly, during distribution. The following is a brief summary:

1. Free money
2. Tax-advantaged money
3. Tax-deferred money
4. Taxable money
   a. Ordinary income
   b. Capital gains and qualified dividends

FREE MONEY

Free money is the best kind of money regardless of tax treatment because, in the end, you have more money than you would have otherwise. Many employers will provide contributions toward employee retirement accounts to offer additional employment benefits and encourage employees to save for their own retirement. With this, employers often will offer a matching contribution in which they contribute up to a certain percentage of an employee's salary (generally three to five percent) toward that employee's retirement account when the employee contributes to their retirement account as well. For example, if an employee earns $50,000 annually and contributes three percent ($1,500) to their retirement account annually, the employer will also contribute three percent ($1,500) to the employee's account. That is $1,500 in free money. Take all you can get! Bear in mind that any employer contribution to a 401(k) will still be subject to taxation when withdrawn.

TAX-ADVANTAGED MONEY

Tax-advantaged money is the next best thing to free money. Although you have to earn tax-advantaged money, you do not have to give part of it away to Uncle Sam. Tax-advantaged money comes in three basic forms that you can utilize during your lifetime; four if prison inspires your future, but we are not going to discuss that option.

One of the most commonly known forms of tax-advantaged money is municipal bonds, which earn and pay interest that could be tax-advantaged on the federal level, or state level, or both. There are several caveats that should be discussed with regard to the notion of tax-advantaged income from municipal bonds. First, you will notice that tax-advantaged has several flavors from the state and federal perspective. This is because states will generally tax the interest earned on a municipal bond unless the bond is offered from an entity located within that state. This severely limits the availability of completely tax-advantaged municipal bonds and constrains underlying risk and liquidity factors. Second, municipal bond interest is added back into the equation for determining your modified adjusted gross income (MAGI) for Social Security. This could push your income above a threshold and subject a portion of your Social Security income to taxation.

In effect, if this interest subjects some other income to taxation then this interest is truly being taxed.

Last, municipal bond interest may be excluded from the regular federal tax system, but it is included for determining tax under the alternative minimum tax (AMT) system. In its basic form, the AMT system is a separate tax system that applies if the tax computed under AMT exceeds the tax computed under the regular tax system. The difference between these two computations is the alternative minimum tax.

TAX-ADVANTAGED MONEY: ROTH IRA

Roth accounts are probably the single greatest tax asset that has come from Congress. They are well known but rarely used. Roth IRAs were first established by the Taxpayer Relief Act of 1997 and named after Senator William Roth, the chief sponsor of the legislation. Roth accounts are simply an account in the form of an individual retirement account or an employer sponsored retirement account that allows for tax-advantaged growth of earnings and, thus, tax-advantaged income.

The main difference between a Roth and a traditional IRA or employer-sponsored plan lies in the timing of the taxation. We are all very familiar with the typical scenario of putting money away for retirement through an employer plan, whereby they deduct money from our paychecks and put it directly into a retirement account. This money is taken out before taxes are calculated, meaning we do not pay tax on those earnings today. A Roth account, on the other hand, takes the money after the taxes have been removed and puts it into the retirement account, so we do pay tax on the money today. The other significant difference between these two is taxation during distribution in later years. Regarding our traditional retirement accounts, when we take the money out later it is added to our ordinary income and is taxed accordingly. Additionally, including this in our income subjects us to the consequences mentioned above for municipal bonds with Social Security taxation, AMT, as well as higher Medicare premiums. A Roth on the other hand is distributed tax-advantaged and does not contribute toward negative impact items such as Social Security taxation, AMT, or Medicare premium increases. It essentially comes back to us without tax and other obligations.

The best way to view the difference between the two accounts is to look at the life of a farmer. A farmer will buy seed, plant it in the ground, grow the crops and harvest it later for sale. Typically, the farmer would only pay tax on the crops that have been harvested and sold. But if you were the farmer, would you rather pay tax on the $5,000 of seed that you plant today or the $50,000 of crops harvested later? The obvious answer is $5,000 of seed today. The truth to the matter is that you are a farmer, except you plant dollars into your retirement account instead of seeds into the earth.

So why doesn't everyone have a Roth retirement account if things are so simple? There are several reasons, but the single greatest reason has been the constraints on contributions. If you earned over certain thresholds (MAGI over $125,000 single and $183,000 joint for 2012), you were not eligible to make contributions, and until last year, if your modified adjusted gross income (MAGI) was over $100,000 (single or joint), you could not convert a traditional IRA to a Roth. Outside these contribution limits, most people save for retirement through their employers and most employers do not offer Roth options in their plans. The reason behind this is because Roth accounts are not that well understood and people have been educated to believe that saving on taxes today is the best possible course of action.

TAX-DEFERRED MONEY

Tax-deferred money is the type of money with which most of people are familiar, but we also briefly reviewed the idea above. Tax-deferred money is typically our traditional IRA, employer sponsored retirement plan or a non-qualified annuity. Essentially, you put money into an investment vehicle that will accumulate in value over time and you do not pay taxes on the earnings that grow these accounts until you distribute them. Once the money is distributed, taxes must be paid. However, the same negative consequences exist with regard to additional taxation and expense in other areas as previously discussed. The cash accumulation value can be used for tax-advantaged income.

TAXABLE MONEY

Taxable money is everything else and is taxable today, later or whenever it is received. These four types of money come down to two distinct classifications: taxable and tax-free. The greatest difference when comparing taxable and tax-advantaged income is a function of how much money we keep after tax. For help in determining what the differences should be, excluding outside factors such as Social Security taxation and AMT, a tax equivalent yield should be used.

TAX-ADVANTAGED IN THE REAL WORLD

To put the tax equivalent yield into perspective, let us look at an example: Rick and Mary are currently retired, living on Social Security and interest from investments and falling within the 25 percent tax bracket. They have a substantial portion of their investments in municipal bonds yielding 6 percent, which is quite comforting in today's market. The tax equivalent yield they would need to earn from a taxable investment would be 8 percent, a 2 percent gap that seems almost impossible given current market volatility. However, something that has never been put into perspective is that the interest from their municipal bonds is subject to taxation on their Social Security benefits (at 21.25 percent). With this, the yield on their municipal bonds would be 4.725 percent, and the taxable equivalent yield falls to 6.3 percent, leaving a gap of only 1.575 percent.

In the end, most people spend their lives accumulating wealth through the best, if not the only vehicle they know, a tax-deferred account. This account is most likely a 401(k) or 403(b) plan offered through our employer and may be supplemented with an IRA that was established at one point or another. As the years go by, people blindly throw money into these accounts in an effort to save for a retirement that we someday hope to reach.

The truth is, most people have an age selected for when they would like to retire, but spend their lives wondering if they will ever be able to actually quit working. To answer this question, you must understand how much money you will have available to contribute toward your needs. *In other words, you need to know what your after-tax income will be during this period.*

All else being equal, it would not matter if you put your money into a taxable, tax-deferred or tax-advantaged account as long as income tax rates never change and outside factors are never an event. The net amount you receive in the end will be the same. Unfortunately, this will never be the case. We already know that taxes will increase in the future, meaning we will likely see higher taxes in retirement than during our peak earning years.

Regardless, saving for retirement in any form is a good thing as it appears from all practical perspectives that future government benefits will be cut and taxes will increase. You have the ability to plan today for efficient tax diversification and maximization of our after-tax dollars during your distribution years.

THE BRANDEIS STORY

Louis Brandeis provides one of the best examples illustrating how tax planning works. Brandeis was Associate Justice on the Supreme Court of the United States from 1916 to 1939. Born in Louisville, Kentucky, Brandeis was an intelligent man with a touch of country charm. He described tax planning this way:

"I live in Alexandria, Virginia. Near the Court Chambers, there is a toll bridge across the Potomac. When in a rush, I pay the dollar toll and get home early. However, I usually drive outside the downtown section of the city and cross the Potomac on a free bridge.

The bridge was placed outside the downtown Washington, D.C. area to serve a useful social service—getting drivers to drive the extra mile and help alleviate congestion during the rush hour.

If I went over the toll bridge and through the barrier without paying a toll, I would be committing tax evasion.

*If I drive the extra mile and drive outside the city of Washington to the free bridge, I am using a legitimate, logical and suitable method of tax avoidance, and I am performing a useful social service by doing so. The tragedy is that **few people know that the free bridge exists.**"*

Like Brandeis, most American taxpayers have options when it comes to "crossing the Potomac," so to speak. It's a financial planner's job to tell you what options are available. You can wait until March to file your taxes, at which time you might pay someone to report and pay the government a larger portion of your income. However, you could instead file before the end of the year, work with your financial professional and incorporate a tax plan as part of your overall financial planning strategy. Filing later is like crossing the toll bridge. Tax planning is like crossing the free bridge.

Which would you rather do?

The answer to this question is easy. Most people want to save money and pay less in taxes. What makes this situation really difficult in real life, however, is that the signs along the side of the road that direct us to the free bridge are not that clear. To normal Americans, and to plenty of people who have studied it, the U.S. tax code is easy to get lost in. There are all kinds of rules, exceptions to rules, caveats and conditions that are difficult to understand, or even to know about. What you really need to know is your options and the bottom line impacts of those options.

ROTH IRA CONVERSIONS

The attractive qualities of Roth IRAs may have prompted you to explore the possibility of moving some of your assets into a Roth account. Another important difference between the accounts is how they treat Required Minimum Distributions (RMDs). When you turn 70 ½ years old, you are required to take a minimum amount of money out of a traditional IRA. This amount is your RMD. It is treated as taxable income. Roth IRAs, however, do not have RMDs, and their distributions are not taxable. Quite a deal, right?

While having a Roth IRA as part of your portfolio is a good idea, converting assets to a Roth IRA can pose some challenges, depending on what kinds of assets you want to transfer. The success of your conversion will all depend on the timing.

You may have heard about converting your IRA to a Roth IRA, but you might not know the full net result on your income. The main difference between the two accounts is that the growth of investments within a traditional IRA is not taxed until income is withdrawn from the account, whereas taxes are charged on contribution amounts to a Roth IRA, not withdrawals. The problem, however, is that when assets are removed from a traditional IRA, even if the assets are being transferred to a Roth IRA account, taxes apply.

There are a lot of reasons to look at Roth conversions. People have a lot of money in IRAs, up to multiple millions of dollars. Even with $500,000, when they turn 70 ½ years old, their RMD is going to be approximately $18,000, and they have to take that out whether they want to or not. It's a tax issue. Essentially, if you will be subject to high RMDs, it could have impacts on how much of your Social Security is taxable, and on your tax bracket.

By paying taxes now instead of later on assets in a Roth IRA, you can realize tax-advantaged growth. You pay once and you're done paying. Your heirs are done paying. It's a powerful tool. Here's a simple example to show you how powerful it can be:

Imagine that you pay to convert a traditional IRA to a Roth. You have decided that you want to put the money in a vehicle that gives you a tax-advantaged income option down the road. If you pay a 25 percent tax on that conversion and the Roth IRA then doubles in value over the next 10 years, you could look at your situation as only having paid 12.5 percent tax.

The prospect of tax-advantaged income is a tempting one. While you have to pay a conversion tax to transfer your assets, you also have turned taxable income into tax free retirement money that you can let grow as long as you want without being required to withdraw it.

There are options, however, that address this problem. Much like the Brandeis story, there may be a "free bridge" option for many investors.

Your financial professional will likely tell you that it is not a matter of whether or not you should perform a Roth IRA conversion, it is a matter of how much you should convert and when.

Here are some of the things to consider before converting to a Roth IRA:

- If you make a conversion before you retire, you may end up paying higher taxes on the conversion because it is likely that you are in some of your highest earning years, placing you in the highest tax bracket of your life. It is possible that a better strategy would be to wait until after you retire, a time when you may have less taxable income, which would place you in a lower tax bracket.
- Many people opt to reduce their work hours from full-time to part-time in the years before they retire. If you have pursued this option, your income will likely be lower, in turn lowering your tax rate.
- The first years that you draw Social Security benefits can also be years of lower reported income, making it another good time frame in which to convert to a Roth IRA.

One key strategy to handling a Roth IRA conversion is to **_always be able to pay the cost of the tax conversion with outside money_**. Structuring your tax year to include something like a significant deduction can help you offset the conversion tax. This way you aren't forced to take the money you need for taxes from the value of the IRA. The reason taxes apply to this maneuver is because when you withdraw money from a traditional IRA, it is treated as taxable income by the IRS. Your financial professional, with the help of the CPAs at their firm, may be able to provide you with options like after-tax money, itemized deductions or other situations that can pose effective tax avoidance options.

Some examples of avoiding Roth IRA conversions taxes include:

- *Using medical expenses that are above 10 percent of your Adjusted Gross Income.* If you have health care costs that you can list as itemized deductions, you can convert an amount of income from a traditional IRA to a Roth IRA that is offset by the deductible amount. Essentially, deductible medical expenses negate the taxes resulting from recording the conversion.
- *Individuals, usually small business owners, who are dealing with a Net Operating Loss (NOL).* If you have NOLs, but aren't able to utilize all of them on your tax return, you can carry them forward to offset the taxable income from the taxes on income you convert to a Roth IRA.
- *Charitable giving.* If you are charitably inclined, you can use the amount of your donations to reduce the amount of taxable income you have during that year. By matching the amount you convert to a Roth IRA to the amount your taxable income was reduced by charitable giving, you can essentially avoid taxation on the conversion. You may decide to double your donations to a charity in one year, giving them two years' worth of donations in order to offset the Roth IRA conversion tax on this year's tax return.
- *Investments that are subject to depletion.* Certain investments can kick off depletion expenses. If you make an investment and are subject to depletion expenses, they can be deducted and used to offset a Roth IRA conversion tax.

Not all of the above scenarios work for everyone, and there are many other options for offsetting conversion taxes. The point is that you have options, and your financial professional and tax professional can help you understand those options.

If you have a traditional IRA, Roth conversions are something you should look at. As you approach retirement you should consider your options and make choices that keep more of your money in your pocket, not the government's.

ADDITIONAL TAX BENEFITS OF ROTH IRAS

Not only do Roth IRAs provide you with tax-advantaged growth, they also give you a tax diversified landscape that allows you to maximize your distributions. Chances are that no matter the circumstances, you will have taxed income and other assets subject to taxation. *But if you have a Roth IRA, you have the unique ability to manage your Adjusted Gross Income (AGI), because you have a tax-advantaged income option!*

Converting to a Roth IRA can also help you preserve and build your legacy. Because Roth IRAs are exempt from RMDs, after you make a conversion from a traditional IRA, your Roth account can grow tax-advantaged for another 15, 20 or 25 years and it can be used as tax-advantaged income by your heirs. It is important to note, however, that non-spousal beneficiaries do have to take RMDs from a Roth IRA, or choose to stretch it and draw tax-advantaged income out of it over their lifetime.

TO CONVERT OR NOT TO CONVERT?

Conversions aren't only for retirees. You can convert at any time. Your choice should be based on your individual circumstances and tax situation. Sticking with a traditional IRA or converting to a Roth, again, depends on your individual circumstances, including your income, your tax bracket and the amount of deductions you have each year.

Is it better to have a Roth IRA or traditional IRA? It depends on your individual circumstance. Some people don't mind having taxable income from an IRA. Their income might not be very high and their RMD might not bump their tax bracket up, so it's not as big a deal. A similar situation might involve income from Social Security. Social Security benefits are taxed based on other income you are drawing. If you are in a position where none or very little of your Social Security benefit is subject to taxes, paying income tax on your RMD may be very easy.

» *There are also situations where leveraging taxable income from a traditional IRA can work to your advantage come tax time. For example, Miles and Alyssa dream of buying a boat when they retire. It is something they have looked forward to their entire marriage. In addition to the savings and invest-ments that they created to supply them with income during retirement, which includes a traditional IRA, they have also saved money for the sole purpose of purchasing a boat once they stop working.*

When the time comes and they finally buy the boat of their dreams, they pay an additional $15,000 in sales taxes that year because of the large purchase. Because they are retired and earning less money, the deductions they used to be able to realize from their income taxes are no longer there. The high amount of sales taxes they paid on the boat puts them in a position where they could benefit from taking taxable income from a traditional IRA.

When Miles and Alyssa's financial professional learns about their purchase, he immediately contacts a CPA at his firm to run the numbers. They determine that by taking a $15,000 distribution from their IRA, they could fulfill their income needs to offset the $15,000 sales tax deduction that they were claiming due to the purchase of their boat. In the end, they pay zero taxes on their income distribution from their IRA.

The moral of the story? ***Having a tax diversified landscape gives you options.*** Having capital assets that can be liquidated, tax-advantaged income options and sources that can create capital gains or capital losses will put you in a position to play your cards right no matter what you want to accomplish with your taxes. The ace up your sleeve is your financial professional and the CPAs they work with. Do yourself a favor and *plan* your taxes instead of *reporting* them!

CHAPTER 9 RECAP //

- A closer examination of the debt ceiling and taxes throughout U.S. history points to the benefits of tax diversification.
- Most people are familiar with tax-deferred methods of retirement savings such a traditional IRAs. By taking action now, you can prepare for the rise in taxes by restructuring your assets to include the benefits of free and tax-advantaged money.
- Tax-advantaged money is money you earn without having to pay taxes on. One of the most common forms includes municipal bonds, but be aware these come with many state and federal caveats and complexities.
- Roth IRAs and life insurance are two forms of tax-advantaged money that can take advantage of today's lower tax rate when preparing for tomorrow's retirement.
- Look for the "free bridge" option in your tax strategy.
- Converting from a traditional to a Roth IRA can provide you with tax-advantaged retirement income.
- Converting to a Roth IRA can also help you preserve and build your legacy.
- There are many ways to reduce your taxes. Being smart about your Roth IRA conversion is one of the main ways to do so.

10

THE NEXT GENERATION

"You will excuse me now, Captain. I have an appointment with eternity, and I don't want to be late."
— Dr. Tolian Soran, *Star Trek: Generations*

If you're like most people, planning your estate isn't on the top of your list of things to do. Planning your income needs for retirement, managing your assets and just living your life without worrying about how your estate will be handled when you are gone make legacy planning less than attractive for a Saturday afternoon task. The fact of the matter, however, is that if you don't plan your legacy, someone else will. That someone else is usually a combination of the IRS and other government entities: lawyers, executors, courts, and accountants. Who do you think has the best interests of your beneficiaries in mind?

Today, there is more consideration given to planning a legacy than just maximizing your estate. When most people think about an estate, it may seem like something only the very wealthy have: a stately manor or an enormous business. But a legacy is something else entirely. A legacy is more than the sum total of the financial assets you have accumulated. It is the lasting impression you make on those you leave behind. The dollar and cents are just a small part of a legacy.

A legacy encompasses the stories that others tell about you, shared experiences and values. An estate may pay for college tuition, but a legacy may inform your grandchildren about the importance of higher education and self-reliance.

A legacy may also contain family heirlooms or items of emotional significance. It may be a piece of art your great-grandmother painted, family photos, or a childhood keepsake.

When you go about planning your legacy, certainly explore strategies that can maximize the financial benefit to the ones you care about. But also take the time to ensure that you have organized the whole of your legacy, and let that be a part of the last gift you leave.

Many people avoid planning their legacy until they feel they must. Something may change in your life, like the birth of a grandchild, the diagnosis of a serious health problem, or the death of a close friend or loved one. Waiting for tragedy to strike in order to get your affairs in order is not the best course of action. The emotional stress of that kind of situation can make it hard to make patient, thoughtful decisions. Taking the time to create a premeditated and thoughtful legacy plan will assure that your assets will be transferred where and when you want them when the time comes.

THE BENEFITS OF PLANNING YOUR LEGACY

The distribution of your assets, whether in the form of property, stocks, Individual Retirement Accounts, 401(k)s or liquid assets, can be a complicated undertaking if you haven't left clear instructions about how you want them handled. Not having a plan will cost more money and take more time, leaving your loved ones to wait (sometimes for years) and receive less of your legacy than if you had a clear plan.

Planning your legacy will help your assets be transferred with little delay and little confusion. Instead of leaving decisions about how to distribute your estate to your family, attorneys or financial professionals, preserve your legacy and your wishes by drafting a clear plan at an early age.

And while you know all that, it can still be hard to sit down and do it. It reminds you that life is short, and the relatively complicated nature of sorting through your assets can feel like a daunting task. But one thing is for sure: *it is impossible for your assets to be transferred or distributed the way you want at the end of your life if you don't have a plan.*

Ask yourself:

- Are my assets up to date?
- Have my primary and contingent beneficiaries been clearly designated?
- Does my plan allow for restriction of a beneficiary?
- Does my legacy plan address minor children that I want to provide with income?
- Does my legacy plan allow for multi-generational payout?

Answers to these questions are critical if you want the final say in how your assets are distributed. In order to achieve your legacy goals, you need a plan.

MAKING A PLAN

Eventually, when your income need is filled and you have sufficient standby money to meet your need for emergencies, travel or other extra expenses you are planning for, whatever isn't used during your lifetime becomes your financial legacy. The money that you do not use during your lifetime will either go to loved ones, unloved ones, charity, or the IRS. The questions is, who would you rather disinherit?

By having a legacy plan that clearly outlines your assets, your beneficiaries and your distribution goals, you can make sure that your money and property is ending up in the hands of the people you determine beforehand. Is it really that big of a deal? It absolutely is. Think about it. Without a clear plan, it is impossible for anyone to know if your beneficiary designations are current and reflect your wishes because you haven't clearly expressed who your beneficiaries are. You may have an idea of who you want your assets to go to, but without a plan, it is anyone's guess. It is also impossible to know if the titling of your assets is accurate unless you have gone through and determined whose name is on the titles. More importantly, *if you have not clearly and effectively communicated your desires regarding the planned distribution of your legacy, you and your family may end up losing a large part of it.*

As you can see, managing a legacy is more complicated than having an attorney read your will, divide your estate and write checks to your heirs. The additional issue of taxes, Family Maximum Benefit calculations and a host of other decisions rear their heads. Educating yourself about the best options for positioning your legacy assets is a challenging undertaking. Working with a financial professional who is versed in determining the most efficient and effective ways of preserving and distributing your legacy can save you time, money and strife.

So, how do you begin?

Making a Legacy Plan Starts with a Simple List. The first, and one of the largest, steps to setting up an estate plan with a financial professional that reflects your desires is creating a detailed inventory of your assets and debts (if you have any). You need to know what assets you have, who the beneficiaries are, how much they are worth and how they are titled. You can start by identifying and listing your assets. This is a good starting point for working with a financial professional who can then help you determine the detailed information about your assets that will dictate how they are distributed upon your death.

If you are particularly concerned about leaving your kids and grandkids a lifetime of income with minimal taxes, you will want to discuss a Stretch IRA option with your financial professional.

STRETCH IRAS: GETTING THE MOST OUT OF YOUR MONEY

In 1986, the U.S. Congress passed a law that allows for multi-gen-erational distributions of IRA assets. This type of distribution is called a Stretch IRA because it stretches the distribution of the account out over a longer period of time to several beneficiaries. It also allows the account to continue accumulating value throughout your relatives' lifetimes. You can use a Stretch IRA as an income tool that distributes throughout your lifetime, your children's lifetimes and your grandchildren's lifetimes.

Stretch IRAs are an attractive option for those more concerned with creating income for their loved ones than leaving them with a lump sum that may be subject to a high tax rate. With traditional IRA distributions, non-spousal beneficiaries must generally take distributions from their inherited IRAs, whether transferred or not, within five years after the death of the IRA owner. An exception to this rule applies if the beneficiary elects to take distributions over his or her lifetime, which is referred to as stretching the IRA.

Let's begin by looking at the potential of stretching an IRA throughout multiple generations.

» *In this scenario, Mr. Cleaver has an IRA with a current balance of $350,000. If we assume a five percent annual rate of return, and a 28 percent tax rate, the Stretch IRA turned a $502,625 legacy into more than $1.5 million. Doubling the value of the IRA also provided Mr. Cleaver, his wife, two children and three grandchildren with income. Not choosing*

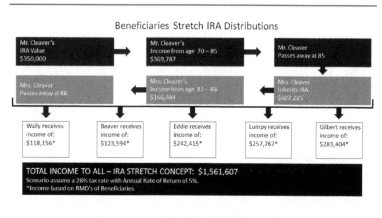

Beneficiaries Stretch IRA Distributions

| Mr. Cleaver's IRA Value $350,000 | Mr. Cleaver's Income from age 70 – 85 $369,787 | Mr. Cleaver Passes away at 85 |
| Mrs. Cleaver Passes away at 88 | Mrs. Cleaver's Income from age 82 – 88 $166,484 | Mrs. Cleaver Inherits IRA $607,285 |

| Wally receives income of: $118,156* | Beaver receives income of: $123,594* | Eddie receives income of: $242,415* | Lumpy receives income of: $257,767* | Gilbert receives income of: $283,404* |

TOTAL INCOME TO ALL – IRA STRETCH CONCEPT: $1,561,607
Scenario assume a 28% tax rate with Annual Rate of Return of 5%.
*Income based on RMD's of Beneficiaries

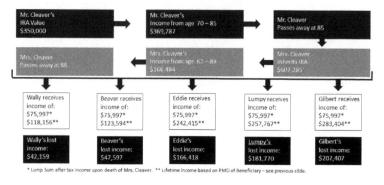

Beneficiaries **FAIL** to Stretch IRA Distributions

| Mr. Cleaver's IRA Value $350,000 | Mr. Cleaver's Income from age 70 – 85 $369,787 | Mr. Cleaver Passes away at 85 |
| Mrs. Cleaver Passes away at 88 | Mrs. Cleaver's Income from age 82 – 88 $166,484 | Mrs. Cleaver Inherits IRA $607,285 |

| Wally receives income of: $75,997* $118,156** | Beaver receives income of: $75,997* $123,594** | Eddie receives income of: $75,997* $242,415** | Lumpy receives income of: $75,997* $257,767** | Gilbert receives income of: $75,997* $283,404** |

| Wally's lost income: $42,159 | Beaver's lost income: $47,597 | Eddie's lost income: $166,418 | Lumpy's lost income: $181,770 | Gilbert's lost income: $207,407 |

* Lump Sum after tax income upon death of Mrs. Cleaver. ** Lifetime income based on RMD of Beneficiary – see previous slide.

the stretch option would have cost nearly $800,000 and had impacts on six of Mr. Cleaver's loved ones.

Unfortunately, many things may also play a role in failing to stretch IRA distributions. It can be tempting for a beneficiary to take a lump sum of money despite the tax consequences. Fortunately, if you want to solidify your plan for distribution, there are options that will allow you to open up an IRA and incorporate "spendthrift" clauses for your beneficiaries. This will ensure your legacy is stretched appropriately and to your specifications. Only certain insurance companies allow this option, and you will not find this benefit with any brokerage accounts. You need to work with a financial professional who has the appropriate relationship with an insurance company that provides this option.

CHAPTER 10 RECAP //

- Your legacy encompasses more than just the physical assets left behind for your children, grandchildren and charities or organizations. It's how you will be remembered.
- Managing a legacy is more complicated than having an attorney read your will, divide your estate, and write checks to your heirs. Issues such as taxes, Family Maximum Benefit calculations and a host of other concerns make it necessary to educate yourself. Working with a financial professional can save you time, money and stress.
- Legacy planning begins with a simple list.

11

YOUR FINAL MISSION:
PREPARING YOUR LEGACY

"Five card stud, nothing wild. And the sky's the limit!"
– Captain Picard, Star Trek: The Next Generation

Captain Picard organized his assets long ago. He started planning his retirement early and made investment decisions that would meet his needs. With a combination of IRA to Roth IRA conversions, a series of income annuities and a well-planned money management strategy overseen by his financial professional, he easily filled his income gap and was able to focus on ways to accumulate his wealth throughout his retirement. He reorganized his Know So and Hope So Money as he got older. When Captain Picard retired, he had an income plan created that allowed him to maximize his Social Security benefit. He even had enough to accumulate wealth during his retirement. At this point, Captain Picard turned his attention to planning his legacy. He wanted to know how he could maximize the amount of his legacy he will pass on to his heirs.

Captain Picard met with an attorney to draw up a will, but he quickly learned that while having a will was a good plan, it wasn't the most efficient way to distribute his legacy. In fact, relying solely on a will created several roadblocks.

The two main problems that arose for Captain Picard were *Probate* and *Unintentional Disinheritance:*

Problem #1: Probate

Probate. Just speaking the word out loud can cause shivers to run down your spine. Probate's ugly reputation is well deserved. It can be a costly, time consuming process that diminishes your estate and can delay the distribution of your estate to your loved ones. Nasty stuff, by any measure. Unless you have made a clear legacy plan and discussed options for avoiding probate, it is highly likely that you have many assets that might pass through probate needlessly. ***If your will and beneficiary designations aren't correctly structured, some of these assets will go through the probate process, which can turn dollars into cents.***

If you have a will, probate is usually just a formality. There is little risk that your will won't be executed per your instructions. The problem arises when the costs and lengthy timeline that probate creates come into play. Probate proceedings are notoriously expensive, lengthy and ponderous. A typical probate process identifies all of your assets and debts, pays any taxes and fees that you owe (including estate tax), pays court fees, and distributes your property and assets to your inheritors. This process usually takes at least a year, and can take even longer before your inheritors actually receive anything that you have left for them. For this reason, and because of the sometimes exorbitant fees that may be charged by lawyers and accountants during the process, probate has earned a nasty reputation.

Probate can also be a painstakingly public process. Because the probate process happens in court, the assets you own that go through a probate procedure become part of the public record. While this may not seem like a big deal to some, other people don't want that kind of intimate information available to the public.

Additionally, if your estate is entirely distributed via your will, the money that your family may need to cover the costs of your medical bills, funeral expenses and estate taxes will be tied up in probate, which can last up to a year or more. While immediate family members may have the option of requesting immediate cash from your assets during probate to cover immediate health care expenses, taxes, and fees, that process comes with its own set of complications. Choosing alternative methods for distributing your legacy can make life easier for your loved ones and can help them claim more of your estate in a more timely fashion than traditional methods.

A simpler and less tedious approach is to avoid probate altogether by structuring your estate to be distributed outside of the probate process. Two common ways of doing this are by structuring your assets inside a life insurance plan, and by using individual retirement planning tools like IRAs that give you the option of designating a beneficiary upon your death.

Problem #2: Unintentionally Disinheriting Your Family

You would never want to unintentionally disinherit a loved one or loved ones because of confusion surrounding your legacy plan. Unfortunately, it happens. Why? This terrible situation is typically caused by a simple lack of understanding. In particular, mistakes regarding legacy distribution occur with regards to those whom people care for the most: their grandchildren.

One of the most important ways to plan for the inheritance of your grandchildren is by properly structuring the distribution of your legacy. Specifically, you need to know if your legacy is going to be distributed *per stirpes* or *per capita*.

Per Stirpes. *Per stirpes* is a legal term in Latin that means "by the branch." Your estate will be distributed *per stirpes* if you designate each branch of your family to receive an equal share of your estate. In the event that your children predecease you, their share will be distributed evenly between their children—your grandchildren.

Per Capita. *Per capita* distribution is different in that you may designate different amounts of your estate to be distributed to members of the same generation.

Per stirpes distribution of assets will follow the family tree down the line as the predecessor beneficiaries pass away. On the other hand, per capita distribution of assets ends on the branch of the family tree with the death of a designated beneficiary. For example, when your child passes away, in a per capita distribution, your grandchildren would not receive distributions from the assets that you designated to your child.

What the terms mean is not nearly as important as what they do, however. The reality is that improperly titled assets could accidentally leave your grandchildren disinherited upon the death of their parents. It's easy to check, and it's even easier to fix.

A simple way to remember the difference between the two types of distribution goes something like this: "***Stirpes are forever and Capita is capped.***"

Another way to avoid complicated legacy distribution problems, and the probate process, is by leveraging a life insurance plan.

LIFE INSURANCE: AN IMPORTANT LEGACY TOOL

One of the most powerful legacy tools you can leverage is a good life insurance policy. Life insurance is a highly efficient legacy tool because it creates money when it is needed or desired the most.

Over the years, life insurance has become less expensive, while it offers more features, and it provides longer guarantees.

There are many unique benefits of life insurance that can help your beneficiaries get the most out of your legacy. Some of them include:

- Providing beneficiaries with a tax-free, liquid asset.
- Covering the costs associated with your death.
- Providing income for your dependents.
- Offering an investment opportunity for your beneficiaries.
- Covering expenses such as tuition or mortgage down payments for your children or grandchildren.

Very few people want life insurance, but nearly everyone wants what it does. Life insurance is specifically, and uniquely, capable of creating money when it is needed most. When a loved one passes, no amount of money can remove the pain of loss. And certainly, money doesn't solve the challenges that might arise with losing someone important.

It has been said that when you have money, you have options. When you don't have money, your options are severely limited. You might imagine a life insurance policy can give your family and loved ones options that would otherwise be impossible.

> » *William spent the last 20 years building a small business. In so many ways, it is a family business. Each of his three children, Maddie, Ruby and Edward, worked in the shop part-time during high school. But after all three attended college, only Maddie returned to join her father, and eventually will run the business full-time when William retires.*
>
> *William is able to retire comfortably on Social Security and on-going income from the shop, but the business is nearly his entire financial legacy. It is his wish that Maddie own the*

business outright, but he also wants to leave an equal legacy to each of his three children.

There is no simple way to divide the business into thirds and still leave the business intact for Maddie.

William ends up buying a life insurance policy to make up the difference. Ruby and Edward will receive their share of an inheritance in cash from the life insurance policy and Maddie will be able to inherit the business intact.

William is able to accomplish his goals, treat all three children equitably and leave Maddie the business she helped to build.

If you have a life insurance policy but you haven't looked at it in a while, you may not know how it operates, how much it is worth and how it will be distributed to your beneficiaries. You may also need to update your beneficiaries on your policy. In short, without a comprehensive review of your policy, you don't really know where the money will go or to whom it will go.

If you don't have a life insurance policy but are looking for options to maintain and grow your legacy, speaking with a professional can show you the benefits of life insurance. Many people don't consider buying a life insurance policy until some event in their life triggers it, like the loss of a loved one, an accident or a health condition.

BENEFITS OF LIFE INSURANCE

Life insurance is a useful and secure tool for contingency planning, ensuring that your dependents receive the assets that you want them to have, and for meeting the financial goals you have set for the future. While it bears the name "Life Insurance," it is, in reality, a diverse financial tool that can meet many needs. The main function of a life insurance policy is to provide financial assets for your survivors. Life insurance is particularly efficient at achieving this goal because it provides a tax-advantaged lump sum of money in the form of a death benefit to your beneficiary or beneficiaries. That financial asset can be used in a number of ways. It can be structured as an investment to provide income for your spouse or children, it can pay down debts, and it can be used to cover estate taxes and other costs associated with death.

LIVING BENEFITS

Many of today's life insurance policies and annuity products also have riders and provisions for increased income in the event of chronic illness. Often known as Living Benefits, these products provide you with the means to pay for home health care or a nursing home facility while you are still alive. With annuities, these benefits are sometimes known as "income doublers" because the fixed income contracted by the rider will double should you or your spouse require long term care. Even if it's too late to qualify for traditional long term care insurance, long term care riders on annuity and life insurance products might still be an option for you, and if you never need long term care, that money is not lost. Instead, your beneficiaries receive a legacy.

TAX BENEFITS

Tax liabilities on the estate you leave behind are inevitable. Capital property, for instance, is taxed at its fair market value at the time of your death, unless that property is transferred to your spouse. If the property has appreciated during the time you owned it, taxation on capital gains will occur. Registered Retirement Savings Plans (RRSPs) and other similarly structured assets are also included as taxable income unless transferred to a beneficiary as well. Those are just a few examples of how an estate can become subject to a heavy tax burden. The unique benefits of a life insurance policy provide ways to handle this tax burden, solving any liquidity problems that may arise if your family members want to hold onto an illiquid asset, such as a piece of property or an investment. Life insurance can provide a significant amount of money to a family member or other beneficiary, and that money is likely to remain exempt from taxation or seizure.

PROTECTION BENEFITS

One of life insurance's most important benefits is that it is not considered part of the estate of the policy holder. The death benefit that is paid by the insurance company goes exclusively to the beneficiaries listed on the policy. This shields the proceeds of the policy from fees and costs that can reduce an estate, including probate proceedings, attorneys' fees and claims made by creditors. The distribution of your life insurance policy is also unaffected by delays of the estate's distribution, like probate. Your beneficiaries will get the proceeds of the policy in a timely fashion, regardless of how long it takes for the rest of your estate to be settled.

Investing a portion of your assets in a life insurance policy can also protect that portion of your estate from creditors. If you owe money to someone or some entity at the time of your death, a creditor is not able to claim any money from a life insurance policy or an annuity, for that matter. As an exception to this rule, if you had already used the life insurance policy as collateral against a loan. If a large portion of the money you want to dedicate to your legacy is sitting in a savings account, investment or other liquid form, creditors may be able to receive their claim on it before your beneficiaries get anything, that is if there's anything left. A life insurance policy protects your assets from creditors and ensures that your beneficiaries get the money that you intend them to have.

HOW MUCH LIFE INSURANCE DO YOU NEED?

Determining the type of policy and the amount right for you depends on an analysis of your needs. A financial professional can help you complete a needs analysis that will highlight the amount of insurance that you require to meet your goals. This type of personalized review will allow you to determine ways to continue providing income for your spouse or any dependents you may have. A financial professional can also help you calculate the amount of income that your policy should replace to meet the needs of your beneficiaries and the duration of the distribution of that income.

You may also want to use your life insurance policy to meet any expenses associated with your death. These can include funeral costs, fees from probate and legal proceedings, and taxes. You may also want to dedicate a portion of your policy proceeds to help fund tuition or other expenses for your children or grandchildren. You can buy a policy and hope it covers all of those costs, or you can work with a professional who can calculate exactly how much insurance you need and how to structure it to meet your goals. Which would you rather do?

AVOIDING POTENTIAL SNAGS

There are benefits to having life insurance supersede the direction given in a will or other estate plan, but there are also some potential snags that you should address to meet your wishes. For example, if your will instructs that your assets be divided equally between your two children but your life insurance beneficiary is listed as just one of the children, the assets in the life insurance policy will only be distributed to the child listed as the beneficiary. The beneficiary designation of your life insurance supersedes your will's instruction. This is important to understand when designating beneficiaries on a policy you purchase. Work with a professional to make sure that your beneficiaries are accurately listed on your assets, especially your life insurance policies.

USING LIFE INSURANCE TO BUILD YOUR LEGACY

Depending on your goals, there are strategies you can use that could multiply how much you leave behind. Life insurance is one of the most surefire and efficient investment tools for building a substantial legacy that will meet your financial goals.

Here is a brief overview of how life insurance can boost your legacy:

- Life insurance provides an immediate increase in your legacy.
- It provides an income tax-advantaged death benefit for your beneficiaries.
- A good life insurance policy has the opportunity to accumulate value over time.
- It may have an option to include long-term care (LTC) or chronic illness benefits should you require them.

If your income needs for retirement are met, you may have extra assets that you want to earmark as legacy funds. By electing to invest those assets into a life insurance policy, you can immediately increase the amount of your legacy. Remember, **life insurance allows you to transfer a tax-advantaged lump sum of money to your beneficiaries. It remains in your control during your lifetime, can provide for your long-term care needs and bypasses probate costs.** And make no mistake, taxes can have a huge impact on your legacy. Not only that, income and assets from your legacy can have tax implications for your beneficiaries, as well.

Here's a brief overview of how taxes could affect your legacy and your beneficiaries:

- The higher your income, the higher the rate at which it is taxed.
- Withdrawals from qualified plans are taxed as income.

- What's more, when you leave a large qualified plan, it ends up being taxed at a high rate.
- If you left a $500,000 IRA to your child, they could end up owing as much as $140,000 in income taxes.
- However, if you could just withdraw $50,000 a year, the tax bill might only be $10,000 per year.

How could you use that annual amount to leave a larger legacy? Luckily, you can leverage a life insurance policy to avoid those tax penalties, preserving a larger amount of your legacy and freeing your beneficiaries from an added tax burden.

» *When Kira turned 70 years old, she decided it was time to look into life insurance policy options. She still feels young, but she remembers that her mother died in early 70s, and she wants to plan ahead so she can pass on some of her legacy to her grandchildren just like her grandmother did for her.*

Kira doesn't really want to think about life insurance, but she does want the security, reliability and tax-advantaged distribution that it offers. She lives modestly, and her Social Security benefit meets most of her income needs. As the beneficiary of her late husband's Certificate of Deposit (CD), she has $100,000 in an account that she has never used and doesn't anticipate ever needing since her income needs were already met.

After looking at several different investment options with a professional, Kira decides that a Single Premium life insurance policy fits her needs best. She can buy the policy with a $100,000 one-time payment and she is guaranteed that it would provide more than the value of the contract to her beneficiaries. If she left the money in the CD, it would be subject to taxes. But for every dollar that she puts into the life

*insurance policy, her beneficiaries are guaranteed at least that dollar plus a death benefit, and all of it will be **tax-free!***
    For $100,000, Kira's particular policy offers a $170,000 death benefit distribution to her beneficiaries. By moving the $100,000 from a CD to a life insurance policy, Kira increases her legacy by 70 percent. Not only that, she has also sheltered it from taxes, so her beneficiaries will be able to receive $1.70 for every $1.00 that she entered into the policy! While buying the policy doesn't allow her to use the money for herself, it does allow her family to benefit from her well-planned legacy.

MAKE YOUR WISHES KNOWN

Estate taxes used to be a much hotter topic in the mid-2000s when the estate tax limits and exclusions were much smaller and taxed at a higher rate than today. In 2008, estates valued at $2 million or more were taxed at 45 percent. Just two years later, the limit was raised to $5 million dollars taxed at 35 percent. The limit has continued to rise ever since. The limit applies to fewer people than before. Estate organization, however, is just as important as ever, and it affects everyone.

Ask yourself:

- Are your assets actually titled and held the way you think they are?
- Are your beneficiaries set up the way you think they should be?
- Have there been changes to your family or those you desire as beneficiaries?

There is more to your legacy beyond your property, money, investments and other assets that you leave to family members, loved ones and charities. Everyone has a legacy beyond money. You also leave behind personal items of importance, your values and beliefs, your personal and family history, and your wishes.

Beyond a will and a plan for your assets, it is important that you make your wishes known to someone for the rest of your personal legacy. When it comes time for your family and loved ones to make decisions after you are gone, knowing your wishes can help them make decisions that honor you and your legacy, and give meaning to what you leave behind. Your professional can help you organize.

Think about your:
- Personal stories / recollections
- Values
- Personal items of emotional significance
- Financial assets

Do you want to make a plan to pass these things on to your family?

WORKING WITH A PROFESSIONAL

Part of using life insurance to your greatest advantage is selecting the policy and provider that can best meet your goals. Venturing into the jungle of policies, brokers and salespeople can be overwhelming, and can leave you wondering if you've made the best decision. Working with a trusted financial professional can help you cut through the red tape, the "sales-speak" and confusion to find a policy that meets your goals and best serves your desires for your money. If you already have a policy, a financial professional can help you review it and become familiar with the policy's premium, the guarantees the policy affords, its performance, and its features and benefits. A financial professional can also help you make any necessary changes to the policy.

» *When Scotty turned 88, his daughter finally convinced him to meet with a financial professional to help him organize his assets and get a legacy in order. Although Scotty is reluctant to let a stranger in on his personal finances, he ends up very glad that he did.*

In the process of listing Scotty's assets and beneficiaries, his professional finds a woman's name listed as the beneficiary of an old life insurance annuity that he owns. It turns out, the woman is Scotty's ex-wife who is still alive. Had Scotty passed away before his ex-wife, the annuities and any death benefits that came with them, would have been passed on to his ex-spouse. This does not reflect his latest wishes.

Things change, relationships evolve and the way you would like your legacy organized needs to adapt to the changes that happen throughout your life. There may be a new child or grandchild in your family, or you may have been divorced or remarried. A professional will regularly review your legacy assets and ask you questions to make sure that everything is up to date and that the current organization reflects your current wishes.

CHAPTER 11 RECAP //

- Legacy planning tools include the creation of wills, trusts, living wills and durable power of attorney for health care considerations. An estate planning attorney can help you with your individual needs.
- Review your current life insurance policies in order to determine if refinancing your life insurance makes sense.
- Life insurance provides for the distribution of tax-free, liquid assets to your beneficiaries and can significantly build your legacy. They can also provide Living Benefits to help you pay for the high costs of medical care while you are still living.
- Working with a financial professional can help you select the policy that best meets your needs.

12

CHOOSING YOUR COMMANDER

"Free advice is seldom cheap."
— Rule 59 of the Ferengi Rules of Acquisition,
Star Trek: Deep Space Nine

From the moment you dip your toes into the retirement planning pool to the point you start swimming laps, your assets organized, your income needs met, and your accumulation and legacy plans in place, working with a professional that you trust can make all the difference in how well your retirement reflects your desires.

It is important to know what you are looking for before taking the plunge. There are many people that would love to handle your money, but not everyone is qualified to handle it in a way that leads to a holistic approach to creating a solid retirement plan.

The distinction being made here is that you should look for someone that puts your interests first and actively wants to help you meet your goals and objectives. Oftentimes, the products someone sells you matter less than their dedication to making sure that you have a plan that meets your needs.

Professionals take your whole financial position into consideration. They make plans that adjust your risk exposure, invest in tools that secure your desired income during retirement and create investment strategies that allow you to continue accumulating wealth during your retirement for you to use later or to contribute to your legacy. If you buy stocks with a broker, use a different agent for a life insurance policy and have an unmanaged 401(k) through your employer, working with a financial professional will consolidate the management of your assets so you have one trustworthy person quarterbacking all of the team elements of your portfolio. Financial products and investment tools change, but the concepts that lie behind wise retirement planning are lasting. In the end, a financial professional's approach is designed for those serious about planning for retirement. *Can you say the same thing about the person that advises you about your financial life?*

It's easy to see how choosing a financial professional can be one of the most important decisions you can make in your life. Not only do they provide you with advice, they also manage the personal assets that supply your retirement income and contribute to your legacy. So, how do you find a good one?

HOW TO FIND A FINANCIAL PROFESSIONAL YOU CAN TRUST

Taking care to select a financial professional is one of the best things you can do for yourself and for your future. Your professional has influence and control of your investment decisions, making their role in your life more than just important. Your financial security and the quality of your retirement depends on the decisions, investment strategies and asset structuring that you and your professional create.

Working with a professional is different than calling up a broker when you want to buy or trade some stock. This isn't a decision that you can hand off to anyone else. You need to bring your time and attention to the table when it comes to finding someone with whom you can entrust your financial life. Separating the wheat from the chaff will take some work, but you'll be happy you did it.

While no one can tell you exactly who to choose or how to choose them, the following information can help you narrow the field:

- You can start by asking your friends, family and colleagues for referrals. You will want to pay particular attention to the recommendations that you get from others who are in your similar financial situation and who have similar lifestyle choices. The professional for the CEO of your company may have a different skill-set than the skill-set of the professional befitting your cousin who has 3 kids and a Subaru like you. Do follow-up research on the Internet as well. Look up the people who have been recommended to you on websites like LinkedIn that show the work history, referrals and experience of the candidates that you find most attractive. You will also learn about the firms with or for whom they work. The investment philosophies and reputations of the companies they work for will tell you a lot about how they will handle your money.

- The other side of the coin, however, is that everyone and their brother has a recommendation about how you should manage your money and who should manage it for you. From hot stock tips to "the best money manager in the state," people love to share good information that makes them look like they are in-the-know. Nobody wants to talk about the bad stock purchases they made, the times they lost money and the poor selections they made regarding financial professionals or stock brokers. If you decide to take a friend or family member's recommendation, make sure they have a substantial, long-term experience with the financial professional and that their glowing review isn't just based on a one-time "win."

- You can also use online tools like the search function of the Financial Planning Association (http://www.fpanet.org/) and the National Association of Personal Financial professionals (http://www.napfa.org/). Most of the professionals listed on these sites do not earn commissions from selling financial products, but are instead paid on a fee-only basis for their services. It is important to understand how your professional is being paid. It is generally considered preferable to work with a fee-based professional who will not have conflicts of interests between earning a commission and acting in your best interests.

- Many professionals may also be brokers or dealers that can earn commissions on things like life insurance, certain types of annuities and disability insurance. These professionals have most likely intentionally overlapped their roles so that if their clients choose to purchase insurance or investment products that require a broker or dealer, those clients won't have to find an additional person to work with. Again, understanding the role of your professional will help you make your determination.

NARROWING THE FIELD

1. Decide on the Type of Professional with Whom You Want to Work. There are four basic kinds of financial professionals. Many professionals may play overlapping roles. It is important to know a professional's primary function, how they charge for their services and whether they are obligated to act in your best interest.

Registered representatives, better known as stockbrokers or bank / investment representatives, make their living by earning commissions on insurance products and investment services. Stockbrokers basically sell you things. The products from which they make the highest commission are sometimes the products that they recommend to their clients. If you want to make a simple transaction, such as buying or selling a particular stock, a registered representative can help you. Although registered representatives are licensed professionals, if you want to create a structured and planful approach to positioning your assets for retirement, you might want to consider continuing your search.

The term "planner" is often misused. It can refer to credible professionals that are CPAs, CFPs and ChFCs to your uncle's next door neighbor who claims to have a lead on some undervalued stock about to be "discovered." A wide array of people may claim to be planners because there are no requirements to be a planner. The term financial planner, however, refers to someone who is properly registered as an investment advisor and serves as a fiduciary as described below.

Financial professionals are the diamonds in the rough. These Registered Investment Advisors are compensated on a fee basis. They do, however, often have licensure as stockbrokers or insurance agents, allowing them to earn commissions on certain transactions. More importantly, **financial professionals are financial fiduciaries, meaning they are required to make financial decisions in your best interest and reflecting your risk tolerance.** Investment Advisors are held to high ethical standards and are highly regarded in the financial industry. Financial professionals also often take a more comprehensive approach to asset management. These professionals are trained and credentialed to plan and coordinate their clients' assets in order to meet their goals or retirement and legacy planning. They are not focused on individual stocks, investments or markets. They look at the big picture, the whole enchilada.

Money managers are on par with financial professionals. However, they are often given explicit permission to make investment decisions without advanced approval by their clients.

Understanding who you are working with and what their title is the first step to planning your retirement. While each of the above-mentioned types of financial professionals can help you with aspects of your finances, it is **financial professionals** who have the most intimate role, the most objective investment strategies and the most unbiased mode of compensation for their services. A financial professional can also help you with the non-financial aspects of your legacy and can help you find ways to create a tax planning strategy to help you save money.

2. Be Objective. At the end of the day, you need to separate the weak from the strong. While you might want a strong personal rapport with your professional, or you may want to choose your professional for their personality and positive attitude, it is more important that you find someone who will give sage advice regarding achieving your retirement goals.

It can be helpful to use a process of elimination to narrow the field of potential professionals. Look into five or six potential leads and cross off your list the ones that don't meet your requirements until only one or two remain. Cross-check your remaining choices against the list of things you need from a professional. Make sure they represent a firm that has the investment tools and products that you desire, and make sure they have experience in retirement planning. That is, after all, the main goal.

Don't be afraid to investigate each of your candidates. You'll want to ask the same questions and look for the same information from everyone you consider so you can then compare them and discern which is best for you. You'll want to take a look at the specific credentials of each professional, their experience and competence, their ethics and fiduciary status, their history and track record, and a list of the services that they offer. The professionals who meet all or most of your qualifications are the ones you will contact for an interview.

Potential professionals should meet your qualifications in the following categories:

- *Credentials:* Look at their experience, the quality of their education, any associations to which they belong and certifications they have earned. Someone who has continued their professional education through ongoing certifications will be more up-to-date on current financial practices compared to someone who got their degree 25 years ago and hasn't done a thing since.

- *Practices:* Look at the track record of your candidates, how they are compensated for their services, the reports and analysis they offer, and their value added services.

- *Services:* Your professional must meet your needs. If you are planning your retirement, you should work with someone who offers services that help you to that end. You want someone who can offer planning, advice on investment strategies, ways to calculate risk, advice on insurance and annuities products, and ways to manage your tax strategy.

- *Ethics:* You want to work with someone who is above board and does things the right way. Vet them by checking their compliance record, current licensing, fiduciary status and, yes, even their criminal record. You never know!

3. Ask for and Check References. Once you have selected two or three professionals that you want to meet, call or email them and ask for references. Every professional should be able to provide you with at least two or three names. In fact, they will probably be eager to share them with you. Most professionals rely on references for validation of their success, quality of services and likability. You should, however, take them with a grain of salt. You have no way to know whether or not references are a professional's friends or colleagues.

It is worth contacting references, however, to check for inconsistencies. Ask each reference the same set of questions to get the same basic information. How long have they been working with the professional? What kind of services have they used and were they happy with them? What type of financial planning did they use the professional for? Were they versed in the type of financial planning that you needed? You can also ask them direct questions to elicit candid responses. What was the full cost of the expenses that your professional charged you? Do the reports and statements you receive come from the same firm? Questions like these can help you get a sense of how well the reference knows their professional and whether or not they are a quality reference.

A good reference is a bit like icing on the cake. It's nice to have them, but nothing speaks louder than a good track record and quality experience. And remember that a good reference, while nice to hear, is relatively cheap. How many times have you heard someone on the golf course or at work telling you how great their stockbroker is? But how many times have you heard about the bad investments or losses they have experienced?

4. Use the Internet. As a final step before picking up the phone and calling your candidates, do some digging to discover if anyone on your list has a history of unlawful or unethical practices, or has been disciplined for any of their professional behavior or decisions. Don't worry, you don't have to hire a private investigator. You can easily find this information on the Financial Industry Regulatory Authority's (FINRA) online BrokerCheck tool: http://www.finra.org/Investors/ToolsCalculators/BrokerCheck/.

You should obviously explore the website of a potential professional and the website of the firm that they represent. The Internet allows you to go beyond the online business card of a professional to gain access to information that they don't control. It may all be good information! Or a brief search of the Internet could reveal a sketchy past. The best part is that the Internet allows you to find helpful information in an anonymous fashion.

Start with Google (www.google.com) and search the name of a potential professional and their firm. Keep your eyes trained on third party sources such as articles, blog posts or news stories that mention the professional. You can also check a professional's compliance records online with the Financial Industry Regulatory Authority (FINRA) and the Securities and Exchange Commission (SEC). If you want to dig deeper, you can combine search terms like "scams," "lawsuits," "suspensions" and "fraud" with a professional's or firm's name to see what information arises. More likely than not, you won't find anything. But if you do, you'll be glad that you checked.

HOW TO INTERVIEW CANDIDATES

After vetting your candidates and narrowing down a list of professionals that you think might be a good fit for you, it's time to start interviewing.

When you meet in person with a professional, you want to take advantage of your time with them. The presentations and information that they share with you will be important to pay attention to, but you will also want to control some aspects of the interview. After a professional has told you what they want you to hear, it's time to ask your own questions to get the specific information you need to make your decision.

Make sure to prepare a list of questions and an informal agenda so that you can keep track of what you want to ask and what points you want the professional to touch on during the interview. Using the same questions and agenda will also allow you to more easily compare the professionals after you have interviewed them all. Remember that these interviews are just that, *interviews*. You are meeting with several professionals to determine with whom you want to work. Don't agree to anything or sign anything during an interview until after you have made your final decision.

It can also be helpful to put a time limit on your interviews and to meet the professionals at their offices. The time limit will keep things on track and will allow structured time for presentations and questions/discussion. By meeting them at their office, you can get a sense of the work environment, the staff culture and attitude, and how the firm does business. If you are unable to travel to a professional's office and must meet them at your home or office, make sure that your interviews are scheduled with plenty of time between so the professionals don't cross each other's paths.

You can use the following questions during an initial interview to get an understanding of how each professional does business and whether they are a good fit for you:\

1. How do you charge for your services? How much do you charge? This information should be easy to find on their website, but if you don't see it, ask. Find out if they charge an initial planning fee, if they charge a percentage for assets under their management and if they make money by selling specific financial products or services. If so, you should follow up by asking how much the service costs. This will give you an idea of how they really make their money and if they have incentive to sell certain products over others. Make sure you understand exactly how you will be charged so there are no surprises down the road if you decide to work with this person.

2. What are your credentials, licenses, and certifications? There are Certified Financial Planners (CFPs), Chartered Financial

Consultants (ChFCs), Investment Advisor Representatives, Certified Public Accountants (CPAs) and Personal Financial Specialists (PFSs). Whatever their credentials or titles, you want to be sure that the professional you work with is an expert in the field relevant to your circumstances. If you want someone to manage your money, you will most likely look for an Investment Advisor. Someone that works with an independent firm will likely have a team of CPAs, CFPs and other financial experts upon whom they can draw. If you like the professional you are meeting with and you think they might be a good fit, but they don't have the accounting experience you want them to have, ask about their firm and the resources available to them. If they work closely with CPAs that are experienced in your needs, it could be a good match.

3. What are the financial services that you and your firm provide? The question within the question here is, "Can you help me achieve my goals?" Some people can only provide you with investment advice, and others are tax consultants. You will likely want to work with someone that provides a complete suite of financial planning services and products that touch on retirement planning, insurance options, legacy and estate structuring, and tax planning. Whatever services they provide, make sure they meet your needs and your anticipated needs.

4. What kinds of clients do you work with the most? A lot of financial professionals work within a niche: retirement planning, risk assessment, life insurance, etc. Finding someone who works with other people that are in the same financial boat as you and who have similar goals can be an important way to make sure they understand your needs. While someone might be a crackerjack annuities cowboy, you might not be interested in that option. Ask follow-up questions that will really help you understand where their expertise lies and whether or not their experience lines up with your needs.

5. May I see a sample of one of your financial plans? You wouldn't buy a car without test driving it, and you should not work with a professional without seeing a sample of how they do business. While there is no formal structure that a financial plan has to follow, the variation between professionals can help you find someone who "speaks your language." One professional may provide you with an in-depth analysis that relies heavily on info graphics and diagrams. Someone else may give you a seven page review of your assets and general recommendations. By seeing a sample plan, you can narrow down who presents information in the way that you desire and in ways that you understand.

6. How do you approach investing? You may be entirely in the dark about how to approach your investments, or you might have some guiding principles. Either way, ask each candidate what their philosophy is. Some will resonate with you and some won't. A good professional who has a realistic approach to investing won't promise you the moon or tell you that they can make you a lot of money. Professionals who are successful at retirement planning and full service financial management will tell you that they will listen to your goals, risk tolerance and comfort level with different types of investment strategies. Working with someone that you trust is critical, and this question in particular can help you find out who you can and who you can't.

7. How do you remain in contact with your clients? Does your prospective professional hold annual, quarterly or monthly meetings? How often do *you* want to meet with your professional? Some people want to check in once a year, go over everything and make sure their ducks are all in a row. If any changes over the previous year or additions to their legacy planning strategy came up, they'll do it on that date. Other people want a monthly update to be more involved in the decision making process and to understand what's happening with their portfolio. You basically need to determine the right degree of involvement for both you and your financial professional. You'll also want to feel out how your professional communicates. Do you prefer phone calls or face-to-face meetings? Do you want your professional to explain things to you in detail or to summarize for you what decisions they've made? Is the professional willing to give you their direct phone number or their email address? More importantly, do you want that information and do you want to be able to contact them in those ways?

8. Are you my main contact, or do you work with a team? This is another way of finding out how involved with you your professional will be, and how often they will meet with you. It is also a way to discover how the firm they represent operates and manages their clients. Some professionals will answer their own phone, meet with you regularly and have your home phone number on speed dial. Others will meet with you once a year and have a partner or assistant check in with you every quarter to give you an update. Other companies take an entirely team-based approach whereby clients have a main contact but their portfolio is handled by a team of professionals that represent the firm. One way isn't better than another, but one way will be best for you. Find out how the professional you are interviewing operates before entering into an agreement.

9. How do you provide a unique experience for your clients? This is a polite way of asking, "Why should I work with you?" A professional should have a compelling answer to this question that connects with you. Their answer will likely touch on their investment philosophy, their communication style and their expertise. If you hear them describing strengths and philosophies that resonate with you, keep them on your list. Some professionals will tell you that they will make investments with your money that match your values, others will say they will maximize your returns and others will say they will protect your capital while structuring your assets for income. Whatever you're looking for in a professional, you will most likely find it in the answer to this question.

This last question you will want to ask *yourself* after you've met with someone who you are considering hiring:

10. Did they ask questions and show signs that they were interested in working with me? A professional who will structure your assets to reflect your risk tolerance and to position you for a comfortable retirement must be a good listener. You will want to pass by a professional who talks non-stop and tells you what to do without listening to what you want them to do. If you felt they listened well and understood your needs, and seemed interested and experienced in your situation, then they might be right for you.

THE IMPORTANCE OF INDEPENDENCE

Not all investment firms and financial professionals are created equal. The information in this book has systematically shown that leveraging investments for income and accumulation in today's market requires new ideas and modern planning. In short, you need innovative ideas to come up with the creative solutions that will provide you with the retirement that you want. Innovation thrives on independence. No matter how good a financial professional is, the firm that they represent needs to operate on principles that make sense in today's economy. Remember, advice about money has been around forever. Good advice, however, changes with the times.

Timing the market, relying on the sale of stocks for income and banking on high treasury and bond returns are not strategies. They aren't even realistic ways to make money or to generate income. Working with an independent agent can help you break free from the old ways of thinking and position you to create a realistic retirement plan.

Working with an independent professional who relies on fee-based income tied to the success of their performance will also give you greater peace of mind. When you do well, they do well, and that's the way it should be. Your independent financial professional will make sure that:

- Your assets are organized and structured to reflect your risk tolerance.
- Your assets will be available to you when you need them and in the way that you need them.
- You will have a lifetime income that will support your lifestyle through your retirement.
- You are handling your taxes as efficiently as possible.
- Your legacy is in order.
- Your Red Money is turned into Yellow Money, and is managed in your best interest.

*» Remember Scott and Janice from Chapter 1? Even though they knew they had Social Security benefits coming, they placed some money in savings and each had a pension or a 401(k). **Before they met with a financial professional, they had no idea what their retirement would look like.** After they met with an agent, they knew exactly what types of assets they had, how much they were worth, how much risk they were exposed to and how they were going to be distributed. They also created an income plan so that they could*

pay their bills every month the moment they retired, and they maximized their Social Security benefit by targeting the year and month they would get the most lifetime benefits. After their income needs were met, they were able to continue accumulating wealth by investing their extra assets to serve them in the future and contribute to their legacy. Their professional also helped them make decisions that impacted their taxes, protecting the value of their assets and allowing them to keep more of their money.

    *This isn't a fairy tale scenario. This is an example of how much you stand to gain by meeting with a financial professional who can help you create a planful approach to your retirement. The concept of Know So and Hope So didn't just apply to their money, it also applied to Scott and Janice. They **hoped** that they would have enough for retirement and that they had worked hard enough and saved enough to maintain their lifestyle. Working with a financial professional allowed them to **know** that their income needs were secured and structured to provide them with income for the rest of their lives and with some money to spare.*

    Now, ask yourself: Is your retirement built on hopes and dreams, or a solid, predictable plan?

IT'S WORTH IT!

Finding, interviewing and selecting a financial professional can seem like a daunting task. And honestly, it will take a good amount of work to narrow the field and find the one you want. In the end, it is worth the blood, sweat and tears. Your retirement, lifestyle, assets and legacy is on the line. The choices you make today will have lasting impacts on your life and the life of your loved ones. Working with someone you trust and know you can rely on to make decisions that will benefit you is invaluable. The work it takes to find them is something you will never regret.

Here is a recap of why working with a financial professional is the best retirement decision you can make:

CHAPTER 12 RECAP //

- A good financial professional puts your needs first. Your risk tolerance, goals, objectives, needs, wants, liquidity concerns and timeline worries should be the focus of the meeting before they try to sell you any products. A plan is only good if it is a good fit for you and your family.
- Finding a financial professional you can trust is imperative, because money isn't just about numbers; it's about the life events and the people that come attached to those numbers.
- To find a professional you can trust, start by asking family and friends for referrals. Make sure to do your due diligence and check out the references of anyone who is recommended to you. Look for resources online such as the Financial Planning Association and the National Association of Personal Financial professionals.
- When interviewing candidates, make sure you understand how they charge for their services. Also look for credentials, licenses and certifications. Ask questions such as: How often do you check in with your clients? May I see a sample of one of your financial plans? And, How do you approach investing? These questions will help ensure that you and your professional are a good fit for each other.

GLOSSARY

ANNUAL RESET *(ANNUAL RATCHET, CLIQUET)* – Crediting methods measuring index movement over a one year period. Positive interest is calculated and credited at the end of each contract year and cannot be lost if the index subsequently declines. Say that the index increased from 100 to 110 in one year and the indexed annuity had an 80 percent participation rate. The insurance company would take the 10 percent gross index gain for the year (110-100/100), apply the participation rate (10 percent index gain x 80 percent rate) and credit 8 percent interest to the annuity. But, what if in the following year the index declined back to 100? The individual would keep the 8 percent interest earned and simply receive zero interest for the down year. An annual reset structure preserves credited gains and treats negative index periods as years with zero growth.

ANNUITANT – The person, usually the annuity owner, whose life expectancy is used to calculate the income payment amount on the annuity.

ANNUITY – An annuity is a contract issued by an insurance company that often serves as a type of savings plan used by individuals looking for long term growth and protection of assets that will likely be needed within retirement.

AVERAGING – Index values may either be measured from a start point to an end point (point-to-point) or values between the start point and end point may be averaged to determine an ending value. Index values may be averaged over the days, weeks, months or quarters of the period.

BENEFICIARY – A beneficiary is the person designated to receive payments due upon the death of the annuity owner or the annuitant themselves.

BONUS RATE – A bonus rate is the "extra" or "additional" interest paid during the first year (the initial guarantee period), typically used as an added incentive to get consumers to select their annuity policy over another.

CALL OPTION *(ALSO SEE PUT OPTION)* – Gives the holder the right to buy an underlying security or index at a specified price on or before a given date.

CAP – The maximum interest rate that will be credited to the annuity for the year or period. The cap usually refers to the maximum interest credited after applying the participation rate or yield spread. If the index methodology showed a 20 percent increase, the participation rate was 60 percent and the maximum interest cap was 10 percent, the contract would credit 10 percent interest. A few annuities use a maximum gain cap instead of a maximum interest cap with the participation rate or yield spread applied to the lesser of the gain or the cap. If the index methodology showed a 20 percent increase, the participation rate was 60 percent and the maximum gain cap was 10 percent, the contract would credit 6 percent interest.

COMPOUND INTEREST – Interest is earned on both the original principal and on previously earned interest. It is more favorable than simple interest. Suppose that your original principal was $1 and your interest rate was 10 percent for five years. With simple interest, your value is ($1 + $0.10 interest each year) = $1.50. With compound interest, your value is ($1 x 1.10 x 1.10 x 1.10 x 1.10 x 1.10) = $1.61. The advantage of compound interest over simple interest becomes greater as each subsequent period passes.

CREDITING METHOD *(ALSO SEE METHODOLOGY)* – The formula(s) used to determine the excess interest that is credited above the minimum interest guarantee.

DEATH BENEFITS – The payment the annuity owner's estate or beneficiaries will receive if he or she dies before the annuity matures. On most annuities, this is equal to the current account value. Some annuities offer an enhanced value at death via an optional rider that has a monthly or annual fee associated with it.

EXCESS INTEREST – Interest credited to the annuity contract above the minimum guaranteed interest rate. In an indexed annuity the excess interest is determined by applying a stated crediting method to a specific index or indices.

FIXED ANNUITY – A contract issued by an insurance company guaranteeing a minimum interest rate with the crediting of excess interest determined by the performance of the insurer's general account. Index annuities are fixed annuities.

FIXED DEFERRED ANNUITY – With fixed annuities, an insurance company offers a guaranteed interest rate plus safety of your principal and earnings ((subject to the claims-paying ability of the insurance company). Your interest rate will be reset periodically, based on economic and other factors, but is guaranteed to never fall below a certain rate.

FREE WITHDRAWALS – Withdrawals that are free of surrender charges.

INDEX – The underlying external benchmark upon which the crediting of excess interest is based, also a measure of the prices of a group of securities.

IRA *(INDIVIDUAL RETIREMENT ACCOUNT)* – An IRA is a tax-advantaged personal savings plan that lets an individual set aside money for retirement. All or part of the participant's contributions may be tax deductible, depending on the type of IRA chosen and the participant's personal financial circumstances. Distributions from many employer-sponsored retirement plans may be eligible to be rolled into an IRA to continue tax-deferred growth until the funds are needed. An annuity can be used as an IRA; that is, IRA funds can be used to purchase an annuity.

IRA ROLLOVER – IRA rollover is the phrase used when an individual who has a balance in an employer-sponsored retirement plan transfers that balance into an IRA. Such an exchange, when properly handled, is a tax-advantaged transaction.

LIQUIDITY – The ease with which an asset is convertible to cash. An asset with high liquidity provides flexibility, in that the owner can easily convert it to cash at any time, but it also tends to decrease profitability.

MARKET RISK – The risk of the market value of an asset fluctuating up or down over time. In a fixed or fixed indexed annuity, the original principal and credited interest are not subject to market risk. Even if the index declines, the annuity owner would receive no less than their original principal back if they decided to cash in the policy at the end of the surrender period. Unlike a security, indexed annuities guarantee the original premium and the premium is backed by, and is as safe as, the insurance company that issued it (subject to the claims-paying ability of the insurance company).

METHODOLOGY *(ALSO SEE CREDITING METHOD)* – The way that interest crediting is calculated. On fixed indexed annuities, there are a variety of different methods used to determine how index movement becomes interest credited.

MINIMUM GUARANTEED RETURN *(MINIMUM INTEREST RATE)* – Fixed indexed annuities typically provide a minimum guaranteed return over the life of the contract. At the time that the owner chooses to terminate the contract, the cash surrender value is compared to a second value calculated using the minimum guaranteed return and the higher of the two values is paid to the annuity owner.

OPTION – A contract which conveys to its holder the right, but not the obligation, to buy or sell something at a specified price on or before a given date. After this given date the option ceases to exist. Insurers typically buy options to provide for the excess interest potential. Options may be American style whereby they may be exercised at any time prior to the given date, or they may have to be exercised only during a specified window. Options that may only be exercised during a specified period are European-style options.

OPTION RISK – Most insurers create the potential for excess interest in an indexed annuity by buying options. Say that you could buy a share of stock for $50. If you bought the stock and it rose to $60 you could sell it and net a $10 profit. But, if the stock price fell to $40 you'd have a $10 loss. Instead of buying the actual stock, we could buy an option that gave us the right to buy the stock for $50 at any time over the next year. The cost of the option is $2. If the stock price rose to $60 we would exercise our option, buy the stock at $50 and make $10 (less the $2 cost of the option). If the price of the stock fell to $40, $30 or $10, we wouldn't use the option and it would expire. The loss is limited to $2 – the cost of the option.

PARTICIPATION RATE – The percentage of positive index movement credited to the annuity. If the index methodology determined that the index increased 10 percent and the indexed annuity participated in 60 percent of the increase, it would be said that the contract has a 60 percent participation rate. Participation rates may also be expressed as asset fees or yield spreads.

POINT-TO-POINT – A crediting method measuring index movement from an absolute initial point to the absolute end point for a period. An index had a period starting value of 100 and a period ending value of 120. A point-to-point method would record a positive index movement of 20 [120-100] or a 20 percent positive movement [(120-100)/100]. Point-to-point usually refers to annual periods; however the phrase is also used instead of term end point to refer to multiple year periods.

PREMIUM BONUS – A premium bonus is additional money that is credited to the accumulation account of an annuity policy under certain conditions.

PUT OPTION *(ALSO SEE CALL OPTION)* – Gives the holder the right to sell an underlying security or index at a specified price on or before a given date.

QUALIFIED ANNUITIES *(QUALIFIED MONEY)* – Qualified annuities are annuities purchased for funding an IRA, 403(b) tax-deferred annuity or other type of retirement arrangements. An IRA or qualified retirement plan provides the tax deferral. An annuity contract should be used to fund an IRA or qualified retirement plan to benefit from an annuity's features other than tax deferral, including the safety features, lifetime income payout option and death benefit protection.

REQUIRED MINIMUM DISTRIBUTION *(RMD)* – The amount of money that Traditional, SEP and SIMPLE IRA owners and qualified plan participants must begin distributing from their retirement accounts by April 1 following the year they reach age 70.5. RMD amounts must then be distributed each subsequent year.

RETURN FLOOR – Another way of saying minimum guaranteed return.

ROTH IRA – Like other IRA accounts, the Roth IRA is simply a holding account that manages your stocks, bonds, annuities, mutual funds and CD's. However, future withdrawals (including earnings and interest) are typically tax-advantaged once the account has been open for five years and the account holder is age 59.5.

RULE OF 72 – Tells you approximately how many years it takes a sum to double at a given rate. It's handy to be able to figure out, without using a calculator, that when you're earning a 6 percent return, for example, by dividing 6 percent into 72, you'll find that it takes 12 years for money to double. Conversely, if you know it took a sum twelve years to double you could divide 12 into 72 to determine the annual return (6 percent).

SIMPLE INTEREST *(ALSO SEE COMPOUND INTEREST)* – Interest is only earned on the principal balance.

SPLIT ANNUITY – A split annuity is the term given to an effective strategy that utilizes two or more different annuity products – one designed to generate monthly income and the other to restore the original starting principal over a set period of time.

STANDARD & POOR'S 500 *(S&P 500)* – The most widely used external index by fixed indexed annuities. Its objective is to be a benchmark to measure and report overall U.S. stock market performance. It includes a representative sample of 500 common stocks from companies trading on the New York Stock Exchange, American Stock Exchange, and NASDAQ National Market System. The index represents the price or market value of the underlying stocks and does not include the value of reinvested dividends of the underlying stocks.

STOCK MARKET INDEX – A report created from a type of statistical measurement that shows up or down changes in a specific financial market, usually expressed as points and as a percentage, in a number of related markets, or in an economy as a whole (i.e. S&P 500 or New York Stock Exchange).

SURRENDER CHARGE – A charge imposed for withdrawing funds or terminating an annuity contract prematurely. There is no industry standard for surrender charges, that is, each annuity product has its own unique surrender charge schedule. The charge is usually expressed as a percentage of the amount withdrawn prematurely from the contract. The percentage tends to decline over time, ultimately becoming zero.

TRADITIONAL IRA – See <u>IRA (Individual Retirement Account)</u>

TERM END POINT – Crediting methods measuring index movements over a greater timeframe than a year or two. The opposite of an annual reset method. Also referred to as a term point-to-point method. Say that the index value was at 100 on the first day of the period. If the calculated index value was at 150 at the end of the period the positive index movement would be 50 percent (150-100/100). The company would credit a percentage of this movement as excess interest. Index movement is calculated and interest credited at the end of the term and interim movements during the period are ignored.

TERM HIGH POINT *(HIGH WATER MARK)* – A type of term end point structure that uses the highest anniversary index level as the end point. Say that the index value was at 100 on the first day of the period, reached a value of 160 at the end of a contract year during the period, and ended the period at 150. A term high point method would use the 160 value – the highest contract anniversary point reached during the period, as the end point and the gross index gain would be 60 percent (160-100/100). The company would then apply a participation rate to the gain.

TERM YIELD SPREAD – A type of term end point structure which calculates the total index gain for a period, computes the annual compound rate of return deducts a yield spread from the annual rate of return and then recalculates the total index gain for the period based on the net annual rate. Say that an index increased from 100 to 200 by the end of a nine year period. This is the equivalent of an 8 percent compound annual interest rate. If the annuity had a 2 percent term yield spread this would be deducted from the annual interest rate (8 percent-2 percent) and the net rate would be credited to the contract (6 percent) for each of the nine years. Total index gain may also be computed by using the highest anniversary index level as the end point.

VARIABLE ANNUITY – A contract issued by an insurance company offering separate accounts invested in a wide variety of stocks and/or bonds. The investment risk is borne by the annuity owner. Variable annuities are considered securities and require appropriate securities registration.

1035 EXCHANGE – The 1035 exchange refers to the section of tax code that allows annuity owners the flexibility to exchange one annuity for another without incurring any immediate tax liabilities. This action is most often utilized when an annuity holder decides they want to upgrade an annuity to a more favorable one, but they do not want to activate unnecessary tax liabilities that would typically be encountered when surrendering an existing annuity contract.

401(K) ROLLOVER – See IRA Rollover

Made in the USA
San Bernardino, CA
23 June 2015